C2 000 004 380633

KU-074-097

TRAVELLERS

THE ITALIAN
LAKES
including MILAN

by
BARBARA AND STILLMAN ROGERS

Written by Barbara and Stillman Rogers, updated by Lara Dunston
Original photography by Stillman Rogers

Published by Thomas Cook Publishing
A division of Thomas Cook Tour Operations Limited.
Company registration no. 3772199 England
The Thomas Cook Business Park, Unit 9, Coningsby Road,
Peterborough PE3 8SB, United Kingdom
Email: books@thomascook.com, Tel: + 44 (0) 1733 416477
www.thomascookpublishing.com

Produced by Cambridge Publishing Management Limited
Burr Elm Court, Main Street, Caldecote CB23 7NU

ISBN: 978-1-84848-089-6

© 2004, 2007 Thomas Co
This third edition © 2009
Text © Thomas Cook Pul
Maps © Thomas Cook Pu

Series Editor: Maisie Fitz
Production/DTP: Steven

Printed and bound in Ita

Cover photography: Fron
© Jon Arnold Images Ltd

Birmingham City LIBRARY Council Tower Hill B42 1LG HH Tel: 0121 464 1948	
C2 000 004 380633	
Askews	Jul-2009
914.52104	£9.99

All rights reserved. No pa
a retrieval system or tran
mechanical, recording or otherwise, in any part of the world, without prior
permission of the publisher. Requests for permission should be made to the
publisher at the above address.

Although every care has been taken in compiling this publication, and the
contents are believed to be correct at the time of printing, Thomas Cook Tour
Operations Limited cannot accept any responsibility for errors or omissions,
however caused, or for changes in details given in the guidebook, or for the
consequences of any reliance on the information provided. Descriptions and
assessments are based on the authors' views and experiences when writing and
do not necessarily represent those of Thomas Cook Tour Operations Limited.

The paper used for this book has been independently certified as having
been sourced from well-managed forests and other controlled sources
according to the rules of the Forest Stewardship Council.
This book has been printed and bound in Italy by Printer Trento S.r.l.,
an FSC certified company for printing books on FSC mixed paper in
compliance with the chain of custody and on products labelling standards.

FSC
Mixed Sources
Product group from well-managed
forests and other controlled sources
Cert no. CQ-COC-000012
www.fsc.org
© 1996 Forest Stewardship Council

Contents

KEY TO MAPS

Province boundaries	[i] Information	★ Start of walk/tour
Museum	♣ Park	Motorway
Church	▲ Mountain	Ancient walls
Railway line	S-26 A-5 Road numbers	

Introduction

Say you are going to Italy and everyone is envious. This land of sunshine, Campari and La Dolce Vita *is at the top of everyone's list. Say you are going to the lakes and Milan, and you immediately become a sophisticated traveller. Clearly you are eschewing the ever-popular Golden Triangle of Rome–Florence–Venice because you have already been there.*

Perhaps you have visited Italy before, or perhaps this is your first trip. It doesn't matter. This is a good place to begin, and as good a place to come back to. Nowhere in Italy – or all of Europe – can claim better scenery than the snow-covered Alps reflected in the deep blue waters of a lake whose steep shores are dotted with pastel-coloured buildings. When these wooded mountainsides give way to steeply soaring rock cliffs, and little white sailing boats drift back and forth in the water below, the view only improves.

Northern Italy is a cultural paradise, with enough music (from grand opera

to jazz), museums, *palazzi* (palaces), art galleries, monumental buildings and fashion design to gratify the most dedicated patron. Its churches are museums in their own right, showcases of architectural styles, historic treasures and works by famous artists.

The Lakes Region is surprisingly large, with good transportation. Travellers can go from the fashion streets of Milan to a home-grown celebration of a fruit harvest in the most rural of mountain villages, all in the same day. They can begin a lazy morning lingering over a cappuccino in a café overlooking Milan's Duomo (cathedral), hop on a train to Como for a scenic boat tour of the lake and be back in Milan in time to change for dinner – or dine beside Lake Como and take a later train.

At the heart of any traveller's experiences in Lombardy is their willingness to join local people in their traditions. This might be simply going to church in a local parish or choosing

the little *trattoria* instead of a famous restaurant. Staying in family-run lodgings is a sure way to share local experiences, whether a farm with agritourism rooms or an elegant old villa where the owner chats with you over a *grappa* after dinner.

Above all, Italians are marked by their heartfelt hospitality and openness. Despite the many centuries that tourists have dutifully trudged upon a town's ancient stones, the Italians will still greet you cheerfully, help you find your way, suggest a favourite place to eat, try to understand your fractured attempts at pronunciation, and be genuinely glad to meet you.

The lake town of Como

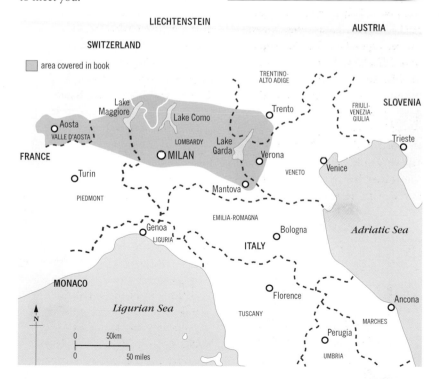

Land and people

The borders separating Italy from its northern neighbours are tangible. The Alps and Dolomites form a solid wall, often a series of walls, so that access is over mountain passes or through tunnels. Historically, such borders were easier to define and defend since they formed a natural barrier that discouraged random mingling.

The same earth-changing forces that shaped these mountains gouged out the lakes that reflect them so prettily. Once the buckling and upheaving of the earth's crust thrust the Alps skywards, glaciers set to grinding them down. It was the glaciers that dug the fjord-like lakes, dropping the debris to form the hills that rise between the lakes and the flat valley of the Po River.

Sunday afternoons find lakeside cafés busy

The largest of the lakes are Garda, Maggiore and Como. South of these, a flat plain stretches from west of Milan to beyond Verona, continuing south to include the Po Valley.

Although the mountains form a wall to the north, the wall is not an even one. Each ridge or chain of peaks is cut and furrowed into a series of long ribs, separated by deep ravines that have been worn by meltwaters from the glaciers. As a result, the Alps lie like a crumpled newspaper. Hidden deep in these valleys are tiny communities, many of which have only recently become accessible by road. Their way of life contrasts sharply with that of the factory worker or banker in Milan – even though only a few dozen kilometres separate them.

The land shapes the people who live in the lakes region in two ways. It governs how they live, since they must choose occupations suited to it and lifestyles that enable them to survive there. Moreover, it governs who will stay and who will move on. Whatever the reason, the people who settled and remained in Italy's Alpine and sub-Alpine regions are an independent lot, self-sufficient and hard-working. The northern way of looking at life, in contrast to the come-what-may attitude of southern Italy, has shaped Milan and Lombardy since the days of Roman Mediolanum. This outlook makes the wheels of Italian industry turn, and keeps its economy working.

History has shaped these northern Italians as well, since it was through here that all the migrations and conquering armies passed – or ebbed and flowed. The population, one could argue, is less 'Italian' and more mixed with Celtic, Lombard, Germanic and other peoples.

However, you will see less visible ethnic diversity in northern Italy than elsewhere in Europe. Not that there isn't plenty of diversity among the Italians themselves, but there are fewer Arabs, Asians and Africans (although numbers are rising). Ethnic diversity lies more in the ways of life between the mountains and the plain, and in the influences of the language and culture of the neighbouring countries. Enter the Valle d'Aosta and you will see the architecture change from stucco to stone and timber, and hear the accents alter until the language becomes a blend of Italian and French. Climb into the mountains of northern Lombardy or the Trentino and you are suddenly in a land of chalets.

Land and people

The tranquil shores of Lake Garda

History

The first known inhabitants of the northern lakes region were prehistoric peoples who lived in caves of the Valpolicella, near Verona, and Valcamonica, near Lake Iseo. Later, the Ligures inhabited the Po Valley, but were overrun by the Celts in the 5th and 4th centuries BC.

280 BC	Roman legions arrive in the Po Valley.
222 BC	Romans take Mediolanum (Milan).
218–200 BC	Second Punic War. Celts push Romans south of Po. Romans regain Mediolanum.
89 BC	Rome grants full citizenship to inhabitants of Verona and Brescia.
15 BC	Mediolanum is made the capital of the Roman 11th region.
AD 313	Edict of Milan. Constantine recognises Christianity.
410	Visigoths invade from the north.
452–93	Attila the Hun sacks Milan. Ostrogoth Theodoric seizes control.
568–71	Lombards conquer north and adopt Christianity.

774	Charlemagne defeats Lombards, and is made King of the Lombards.
1155	Frederick Barbarossa is crowned Holy Roman Emperor.
1162	Barbarossa lays siege to Milan.
1277	Visconti rule of Milan begins.
1559	Spain gains control over Milan region.
1706	Austrians occupy Milan.

The Visconti family ruled Milan from 1277 to 1477

1796	Milan occupied by the French under Napoleon, crowned King of Italy in 1805.		at Salò on Lake Garda.
1814	Austria regains Lombardy.	1944	Italy joins Allies; Italian partisans battle Nazis in occupied areas.
1831	Giuseppe Mazzini founds Young Italy movement, beginning the resistance to Austria.	1946	Vittorio Emanuele III abdicates. Republic of Italy declared.
1848	First War of Italian Independence against Austrian rule fails.	1957	Italy joins European Economic Community, forerunner of the European Union (EU).
1859	Second War of Italian Independence. Battle of Solferino leads to founding of Red Cross.	1970–85	Red Brigades terrorise Milan and other power centres.
1861	Vittorio Emanuele II is crowned King of Italy.	1990s	Kickback scandals rock Milan's economic and political world.
1870	Unification of the Kingdom of Italy is completed.	2002	Italy adopts the euro.
1915	Italy joins Allies in World War I against Germany.	2006	Winter Olympics in Turin attract world attention.
1936	Hitler and Mussolini sign the Axis pact.	2006	After five years in office, rightist Prime Minister Silvio Berlusconi is replaced by left-of-centre Romano Prodi.
1940	Italy joins World War II as a German ally.	2008	Silvio Berlusconi re-elected as Prime Minister.
1943	Mussolini deposed, sets up puppet state	2015	Milan hosts Expo 2015.

Politics

Italy is a parliamentary republic, under a constitution adopted in 1948. It has a president and two legislative houses. The country is divided into 20 regions, whose governments have administrative powers, and those regions are further broken down into 94 provinces.

This book covers most of the region of Lombardy, with parts of Piedmont, the Valle d'Aosta and the Veneto, and a small corner of the Trentino-Alto Adige. The top portion of Lago Maggiore and the central section of Lago di Lugano lie in Switzerland, and are included as well.

While political boundaries within a country usually do not greatly concern leisure travellers, it is handy to know that most tourism matters are administered by region. For example, a directory listing agritourism establishments will probably categorise them under Lombardy or the Veneto, and so it helps to know what region you are in.

To complicate the traveller's life further, each province and each city has its own tourism brochures, tour maps and even offices. If the office belongs to the town (often called *pro loco*), it may have little information about the town's neighbours.

The larger lakes – Garda and Maggiore – are the dividing lines for regions, and so a trip around the lake will mean shifting from one set of tourist information to another and back again before the day is finished.

Garibaldi, Italy's founding father

One thing you may notice while travelling in Italy is the strong sense of regional identity. Perhaps this stems from the fact that, until it was unified in the 1860s, Italy was a series of small independent cities and states. It also reflects genuine differences in the regions.

Politics

Lake Garda straddles three regions: Lombardy, the Veneto and Trentino-Alto Adige

The Romans in northern Italy

As early as the 3rd century BC, the Romans had pushed their northern borders across the Po Valley and founded Mediolanum. The heart of this settlement – its forum – is now Milan's Piazza San Sepolcro, behind the Ambrosiana Museum. The Punic Wars pushed the boundaries this way and that, but, by the late 1st century AD, the Romans were secure enough to make Mediolanum the capital of their newest region.

By then other cities had begun to flourish. In the 1st century BC, residents of Brixia (Brescia) gained Roman citizenship. Augusta Praetoria (Aosta), on the Roman road to Gaul, grew from a legion way station to a city so thriving that it was known as the Rome of the Alps.

By the late 1st century AD, Verona already had a population large enough to build an arena seating more than 20,000 people. A grand villa was built on the point of Sirmione on Lake Garda, and Romans colonised Lake Como's shores.

Not much of the Roman presence is visible in Milan. Some carved stone pieces have been incorporated into Porta Nuova, and the only remaining segment of the Roman wall is visible in the courtyard of the Civico Museo Archeologico (*see pp30–31*).

Evidence of the Romans has fared better elsewhere. Aosta has much of its Roman theatre only because the standing wall was incorporated into other buildings, thus sealing and supporting it. Stripped of its covering for at least half a century, the theatre is again covered, this time in scaffolding while structural repairs are

The excavated ruins of a Roman theatre in Aosta

Verona's ancient Roman forum

Verona preserves its arena, one of the three finest remaining, and the theatre overlooking a Roman bridge that was reconstructed after being damaged in World War II. Portions of a Roman city gate have been exposed under the pavement near Piazza delle Erbe, an entire section of which had been hidden for centuries in the wall of a building. Corso Porta Borsari, Roman Verona's high street, still passes through the 1st-century gate of Porta Borsari. Another 1st-century Roman gate, Arco dei Gavi, stands nearby, moved here along with the stone pavement that was beneath it, complete with chariot tracks (see p141).

Brescia's forum, amphitheatre and Capitolium Temple have been uncovered and partially restored. Although there is more of the restoration than the original, in the Capitolium, it is clear what is original, and the reconstruction gives a good picture of how the structures looked – far better than a row of fragments would. Other Roman treasures in Brescia, including an exquisite mosaic floor, are in the Civici Musei (see p106).

made to save it. The stage, entrance and seating sections fill a large area before the standing wall, all excavated. A Roman bridge and the impressive Arch of Augustus, built in 25 BC, remain, as do other arches, gates and portions of the original walls (see p50).

Elsewhere in the Valle d'Aosta are Roman bridges at St Martin and St Vincent and an aqueduct at Pondel, as well as an arch over a section of Roman road at Donnas.

No one knows exactly how much more of ancient Rome lies buried under pavements and grass or sealed inside buildings, but each new construction project turns up more pieces in the historic jigsaw puzzle.

Culture

Think of the great names in the arts that are associated with Milan, Lombardy and the surrounding regions. Verdi, Donizetti and Toscanini in music; Leonardo da Vinci and Bramante – artist and architect of the Renaissance; and the two great schools of architecture in the Middle Ages, the maestri comacini *and the* maestri campionese. *And less familiar outside of Italy only because of the language difference, Manzoni and d'Annunzio in literature.*

Consider the great arts venues of both La Scala – dream stage for every opera singer – and Verona's arena, home to one of Europe's top three opera festivals. Add to that the superb clothing designers that have put Milan centre stage in fashion.

Wherever you travel in Milan and throughout the Lakes Region, you will

A beekeeper displays his honey in Lazise

find posters for concerts, many of which are free. These are held in churches (often with extraordinary acoustics), parks, palaces, *piazze* (squares) and even at the lakeside, and may feature a local quintet, a visiting choir or a fully fledged concert orchestra. Tourist offices will usually have fliers or listings.

As important as the 'high' culture of the arts and design world is the popular culture that reaches into the soul of every Italian. Here traditions go deep, and local festivals still celebrate triumphs and deliverances from half a millennium ago. The simple rhythms of life and seasons are celebrated in festivals for just about every crop that is grown here, from cherries to wine.

Deep in a valley of the Gran Paradiso each September, farmers bring their best cows to the Battle of the Queens where the winners are awarded coveted decorated bells. In Mantova in May, a medieval wedding is remembered with a costumed parade and flag-

A farmer with his entry in the annual Battle of the Queens show

throwing, while local food producers give out samples of farm sausages and traditional cakes.

Each city, town and village has its saint's day to observe, with statues on parade, the local harvest to be thankful for, and local heroes to remember. It is not like the Italians to do these things quietly or without a party. Tents and temporary bandstands and dance floors will be thrown up in the square, food will be sold or given away, bands will play, and people will wear costumes.

Spring and autumn are the best times to find these festivals, and reading local posters will point you in the right direction. Most are on at weekends, so watch for signs during the week and choose one to visit. Local tourist offices can suggest others, and often publish a listing of events. One tip: the smaller the village and the more local the celebration, the more fun you will have and the more likely it is that you will soon become an 'insider' and join in.

Festivals and events

From the world-renowned opera festival in Verona's Roman arena to the smallest local celebration of the harvest, Italians love an excuse to gather for music, food, wine, shopping and a good time. For the traveller, these are good opportunities to join local people and become a part of their world.

January
Mezzanotte di Fiaba, *Riva del Garda (New Year's Eve, fireworks)*
Natale nel Garda Trentino, *Garda Trentino (Concerts, entertainment and handicrafts)*
Wise Men Procession, *Milan*

February
Carnevale di Milano, *Milan*
Carnevale di Verona, *Verona*
LP record fair at Parco di Esposizione, *Segrate*

March
Gran Carnevale di Arco, *Arco (February or March)*
Oggi Aperto, *Milan (Milan Palazzi open house)*
Trofeo Città di Arco, *Arco (International youth football tournament, February into March)*

April
Liberation Day, *throughout the region*
Liberation Festival, *Peschiera*

Palio del Recioto, *Negrar*
Stramilano, *Milan (In-town race, streets are closed)*

May
Antica Fiera dei Mangiari, *Mantova (Local produce, medieval dress)*
Concert, Sports at Idroscalo Park, *Linate (May to September)*
Cortili Aperti, *Milan (Private courtyard open house)*
Festa del Carroccio, *Legnano (Parade commemorating 1176 battle, costumes)*
Medieval White Wine Festival, *Soave*
Pittori sul Naviglio, *Milan (Art exhibition along the Naviglio River)*
Short Formats Festival, *Milan (Pan-European contemporary dance)*
Square of Flavours, *Verona (Three-day festival of local produce and wines)*

June
Festa del Naviglio, *Milan (Concerts, art, sports, cooking, antique market)*
Festa di of San Giovanni, *Isola Comacina (Fireworks)*

Garda-Trentino Jazz Festival, *Riva del Garda*

Giro Italia, *Milan (Bike race finals)*

Milano d'estate, *Milan (Concerts in Parco Sempione, June–August)*

Opera, *Arena di Verona (Performances through to August)*

Sagra di San Cristoforo, *Milan (Feast of the patron saint of drivers)*

St Peter's Day, *Limone sul Garda (Fair, celebrations, fireworks)*

July

Drodesera Fies, *Centrale di Fies, Drodesera (Festival of avant-garde dance and theatre, into August)*

Fireworks Spectacular, *Sesto Calende*

Notturni in Villa, *Milan (Concerts in city villas)*

Verona Vinorum, *Verona (Wine festival)*

August

Ferragosto, *throughout the region (Feast of the Assumption, public holiday, various celebrations)*

Festival del Film di Locarno, *Locarno (Open-air screening in Piazza Grande, ten days)*

Honey and Apiary Festival, *Bosco Chiesanuova*

Rustico Medioevo, *Canale di Tenno (Riva del Garda) (Medieval dance and folklore)*

September

Battaglia delle Regine, *Cogne, Valle d'Aosta (Cattle show after their return from summer pasture)*

Festival Milano, *Milan (Festival of contemporary music, dance, theatre, new media, continues through October)*

Grape Festival, *Soave*

Italian Formula One Grand Prix, *Monza*

October

Bardolino Wine Festival, *Bardolino*

Chestnut Festival, *San Mauro di Saline*

Festival Milano, *Milan (Festival of contemporary music, dance, theatre, new media)*

Honey Festival, *Lazise*

Italian Fashion Design Show, *Milan (Not open to the public, but a host of other activities occur)*

Luoghi e Sapori in Terra Bresciana *(Festival of local food and wines)*

Maratona di Verona, *Verona (Marathon)*

Marble Exposition, *Verona*

Milan International Film Festival, *Milan*

November

Ancient Snail Fair, *Sant'Andrea-Badia Calavena (Snail market, exhibition, truffles, food and crafts)*

Tutti Santi, *throughout the region (All Saints' Day, public holiday)*

December

Festa di Sant'Ambrogio, *throughout the region (7 December, public holiday)*

Festa dell'Immacolata, *throughout the region (8 December, public holiday)*

Milano Marathon, *Milan*

Stalls of Santa Lucia, *Verona (Christmas fair in Piazza Bra)*

Impressions

Milan is a large, sprawling and often confusing city, and not one that visitors tend to fall in love with at first sight. However, it is well worth seeing and getting to know. The largest city in northern Italy, Milan is also the most culturally exciting, and a mecca for shoppers.

Arriving in Milan

Northern Italy's major international airport is Malpensa, north of Milan, although many flights from within Europe arrive at Milan's smaller (and closer) Linate.

From the airport

Malpensa is roughly halfway between Milan and Lake Maggiore. Travellers bound for Como or Maggiore can go directly from the airport via express buses or by train from Milan's Centrale railway station. Express buses also connect to Milan's Centrale every 30 minutes from Malpensa, and every 20 minutes from Linate. This is the most convenient and least expensive way to get to Milan, although not necessarily the fastest.

Car hire

Major international rental companies are represented at Malpensa for pick-up and delivery. All car rental firms are in Terminal 1. Most companies require a credit card, even if the hire has been prepaid. Before leaving the car park, make sure that you have all the registration and insurance documents, and that you know how to operate the vehicle. Don't plan a long day's driving after a long flight, especially if you are unfamiliar with driving on the right.

If you are leasing a car from Renault (*see p180*), you can arrange to have it delivered to you at Malpensa for an extra charge. It is worth paying to avoid having to drive in Milan, particularly upon arrival.

WARNING

As in any airport, it is important to keep hold of your luggage at all times in Malpensa. More of a problem, however, is protecting your luggage when it emerges from under the bus in Milan. The best precaution is to be among the first off the bus, waiting for your bag when it appears.

Right-hand drive

The most immediate driving problem is the right-hand driving for those from left-hand drive countries, such as the UK and South Africa. In normal traffic, it soon begins to seem natural as you follow other drivers. But at roundabouts or on dual carriageways, it becomes more difficult because your natural instincts give you the wrong signals. Be especially alert and continue to remind yourself of this danger. Ask a passenger to keep watch and remind you, at least until it becomes customary.

Entering Milan

In order to cut down on the amount of traffic in the city, a system of zones has been introduced. The city is divided into wedge-shaped areas within the ring road, and, while you can enter and exit any sector from the ring road, you should leave that section and go around the ring road in order to enter another section. Thus, it is important to know where you are going before you enter the city.

Reserved lanes

In Milan, and occasionally elsewhere, there may be a lane reserved for buses, trams and taxis only. These are marked on the pavement, but are sometimes hard to see at night or if cars are close together in traffic.

Parking

Many car parks have coin-operated ticket dispensers. These are quite simple

The Duomo, Milan's 19th-century Gothic masterpiece

to use, and most have English instructions. In some places, tickets should be bought at nearby newsstands. Put the ticket inside the windscreen so that it is visible from the outside. Some car parks are free, but have a limited stay of an hour or two. You can buy a paper 'clock' at newsstands, or write the time you arrive on a piece of paper.

Parking garages usually have a cashier on site. Take a time-stamped ticket when you enter and keep it with you. Before leaving, pay for the ticket at the *cassa* (cashier window), drive your vehicle to the exit and then insert the ticket to open the gate.

Impressions

Milan's transport system

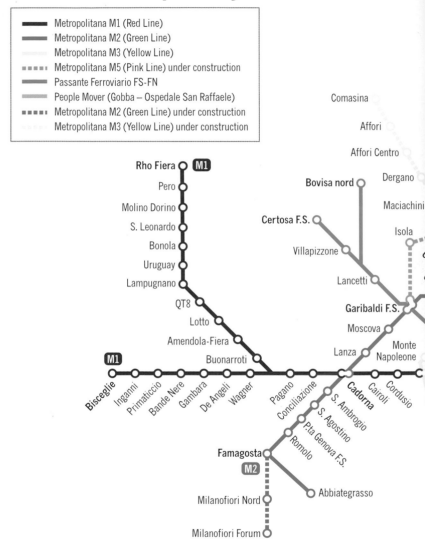

- ▬ Metropolitana M1 (Red Line)
- ▬ Metropolitana M2 (Green Line)
- ▬ Metropolitana M3 (Yellow Line)
- ▪▪▪▪ Metropolitana M5 (Pink Line) under construction
- ▬ Passante Ferroviario FS-FN
- ▬ People Mover (Gobba – Ospedale San Raffaele)
- ▪▪▪▪ Metropolitana M2 (Green Line) under construction
- ▪▪▪▪ Metropolitana M3 (Yellow Line) under construction

Travelling by boat and train

It is particularly appealing to explore the lakes by boat. Not only can you enjoy the best views of shore towns from the water, but the most convenient approach is by boat since most attractions are near the docks. And embarking on a boat, even a mundane car ferry, gives a trip an air of adventure.

Two basic kinds of boat ply the lakes: hydrofoils (*aliscafi*) and traditional lake 'steamers', which no longer operate on steam but retain the name. Hydrofoils are fast and especially good for long-distance trips, but they are not ideal for those who want to take photographs from the deck or enjoy leisurely views of lake scenery.

Rail connections in Italy are frequent, convenient and punctual. Milan is a hub for several main railway lines and a number of smaller lines, including one that shuttles between Milan's Stazione Nord and Como's Milano Nord station, which is right at the boat docks. Train times on this line are designed to coincide with the boat schedule.

Stresa and Ancona (on Lake Maggiore), Lugano and Como are on major international railway lines between Switzerland and Milan. Garda is on the main Milan–Venice line and can be reached by a single connection off the rail route from Innsbruck, Austria.

Train stations are either a short walk from the boat landings or can be reached by frequent local buses or taxi, making it easy to travel to a base anywhere on the major lakes without a car. Once on the lake, boats connect to all other lake towns.

For information and schedules, contact: Navigazione Lago di Como, Piazza Cavour. Tel: (031) 579 211; www.navigazionelaghi.it

Funicular lines climb lakeside mountains for sweeping views

Excursion boats provide scenic tours and access to lake towns

Navigazione del Lago di Lugano.
Tel: (091) 923 1779;
www.lakelugano.ch
Navigazione Lago Maggiore.
Tel: (800) 551 801;
www.navigazionelaghi.it
Navigazione Lago di Garda.
Tel: (030) 914 9511;
www.navigazionelaghi.it

Money-saving passes

Holders of non-European passports can buy a variety of Eurail passes that make train travel more economical and easier. Many of these offer the flexibility of multi-day use over a period of a week or two (*www.eurail.com*). Likewise, each lake's navigation company offers a pass that allows one day's or several days' travel for a fixed price. In each case, it is wise to consider your intended routes and decide if the pass will be cheaper than individual tickets.

Mountain tramways

Providing a different perspective on the lakes, several mountain tramways can lift you from lake towns to a bird's-eye level and Alpine views. An aerial cable car (*funivia*) carries passengers from Stresa's Lido dock (Lake Maggiore) to the summit of Monte Mottarone, stopping at scenic Alpine gardens on the way (*see p55*). From Malcesine, on Lake Garda, a new rotating *funivia* climbs Monte Baldo for views and another Alpine garden (*see p118*).

A venerable tram car (*funicolare*) leaves Como, close to the Milano Nord railway station and the boat landing, to reach the panoramic mountain village of Brunate (*see p82*). On Lake Lugano, a similar two-stage *funicolare* climbs Monte San Salvatore from Paradiso, which can be reached by both boat and train (*see p71*).

Milan

Smart, busy, self-confident, prosperous and a little bit cocky, Milan is the unofficial capital of Italy. The government may be in Rome, but the strings are pulled from here. At least the purse strings are, for Milan is the country's commercial and economic epicentre. And, in the high-wire world of fashion, Milan is the capital of all Europe. All but Parisians (and even some of them) look to Milan's catwalks to see it first.

While Milan is the arrival point for most travellers to northern Italy, and the goal of business people attending the many major trade shows at the Fiera di Milano, it is not a major destination for tourists. Most swing through to see *The Last Supper* and the Duomo, or to shop, but tend to ignore its many other attractions.

Although the city sprawls over an increasing area of the Po plain, most of its historical and artistic sights are

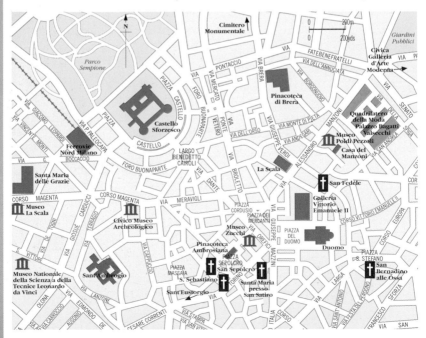

within a reasonable walk from the Duomo, which is – and should be – everyone's first stop. Even the fashion houses of the Quadrilatero della Moda (Fashion Quarter) are only a few blocks from the cathedral's stony frills and leering gargoyles.

Within 2.5sq km (a square mile) are eye-boggling art collections, the world's most famous opera house, historic churches that are art museums in their own right, smart shops and a Renaissance castle. Leonardo da Vinci, Verdi, Caruso, Armani and a chapelful of saints have all worked in this golden mile. St Augustine was baptised under what is now the pavement of thePiazza del Duomo, Napoleon was crowned King of Italy inside the church, Toscanini conducted at La Scala and Verdi died just around the corner. It is no wonder that Milan has a bit of a superiority complex.

A statue of Vittorio Emanuele II in the Piazza del Duomo

Castello Sforzesco

Connected to Piazza del Duomo by the wide Via Dante, Castello Sforzesco makes an elegant home for a group of city museums. Its construction and embellishment spanned a century from the 1360s to the 1450s, with some creative reconstruction at the turn of the 20th century. The Dukes of Milan hired the very best to work here, including Bramante and Leonardo da Vinci.

When the Spanish had control of Milan in the 16th and 17th centuries, they built fortifications around the outside of the castle walls. By the time Napoleon came to town, the walls had deteriorated badly and he ordered them to be torn down immediately.

If the museums are closed, a walk through the castle is still worthwhile since a number of its attractions are visible. Inside the loggia of the **Corte Ducale** are frescoes, and in the Cortile della Rocchetta, opposite, is a glass-housed display of architectural and ornamental stone carving.

In Piazza Castello an impressive fountain can be found, fondly dubbed the *tort de' spus* (wedding cake) by the Milanese.

Museo d'Arte Antica

Particularly outstanding are the collections of sculpture from the Middle Ages and Renaissance. Michelangelo's last work, the *Pietà Rondanini*, in progress when he died, is the attention-getter. However, the Busti tomb sculptures are also Renaissance masterpieces. Many of the works here were saved from churches and convents that were being demolished. *Tel: (02) 8846 3731.*

The 'wedding cake' fountain

Medieval house façades in the castle walls

Museo d'Arte Antica Armeria

Weaponry and armour collections are arranged to show how armour changed to match the technology of weaponry. The rooms of this section are joined by magnificent carved marble arches. *Tel: (02) 8846 3660.*

Museo delle Arti Decorative

Filling galleries off two courtyards, this wide-ranging museum has displays of clocks, ironwork, ceramics, wooden sculpture, ivory, jewellery and Italy's largest collection of furniture. The 12 Trivulzio tapestries are considered the foremost masterpieces of Renaissance textiles. The origins of Milan's pre-eminence in fashion are explored in a collection of costumes, beginning with the 17th century.

Musei dei Castello Sforzesco, Piazza Castello. Open: Tue–Sun 9am–5.30pm. Castle grounds open daily 8am–8pm. Admission charge. Metro: Cadorna or Cairoli. The castle is undergoing major restoration, so portions are closed from time to time. The tourist office has a brochure, 'MilanoMusei', detailing the updated status.

Museo degli Strumenti Musicali

From pocket-sized violins and medieval lutes to hurdy-gurdies, this museum combines the technology of sound with the artistry of fine wood and metal crafts. A rare 1520 instrument is one of the earliest surviving.

Museo della Preistoria e Protostoria

Palaeolithic, Neolithic and Iron Age artefacts, especially those from the Po Valley, are the focus. *Tel: (02) 8846 3702.*

Pinoteca

Paintings from medieval times through to the 18th century include works of Mantegna, Bellini, Lotto and Canaletto. The 20th-century art collection, one of Europe's best, features Picasso and his contemporaries. *Tel: (02) 8846 3731.*

Walk: The Duomo

The first Duke of Milan commissioned Italy's grandest Gothic cathedral before his death in 1402, stirred into action at the prodding of the Archbishop. The third-largest Christian church in the world and the artistic apex of the flamboyant Gothic, Milan's Duomo is almost encrusted with statuary. Dozens of delicately carved spires laden with stone curlicues reach skyward from its roof.

1 Entrance

The bronze panels covering the central doors, although started in the mid-1800s, were not completed until 1965; the middle one of these five doors is bordered with an exquisitely carved bas-relief of flora and fauna. Inside, the 52 soaring columns of the nave and aisles draw your eyes upward to the vaulted ceiling.
Turn right to the kiosk for tickets, returning to the passageway beside the central door.

2 Palaeo-Christian Baptistery

Excavations beneath the *piazza* disclose the circular **Baptistery of San Giovanni alle Fonti**, where St Ambrose baptised St Augustine in AD 387. Some mosaics and patterned marble floor remain, and glass cases show stone carving and other artefacts discovered here and in the adjoining **Basilica di Santa Tecla** excavations.
Return to the nave and turn right to the south aisle.

3 Bishop d'Intimiano Sarcophagus

In the first of the elaborately corniced side altars, the sarcophagus is a fine example of 11th-century stonework. Note the 15th- and 16th-century stained-glass windows in the first chapels along this aisle, the cathedral's oldest.

4 Medici tomb

In the south transept is the tomb of Gian Giacomo de' Medici, by the 16th-century sculptor Leone Leoni. His muse

Bronze panels decorate the Duomo's central doors

was clearly Michelangelo. The transept, or crossing, where two grand altars face each other, is a good place to admire the rows of statues that sit on top of the nave's columns.

Continue around the outer wall, past the startlingly realistic St Bartholomew, into the semicircular ambulatory.

5 Crypt

Below the high altar is the tomb of San Carlo Borromeo (*see pp60–61*). If the crypt is not open, there are good views into it from the ambulatory.

6 Ambulatory windows

The brilliant stained-glass windows enclosing the apse are the work of the brothers Bertini, crafted in the 19th century. Representing biblical scenes, the windows are some of the finest examples of the refinement that the art had reached.

Continue around to the steps ascending to the high altar.

7 Choir

Behind the high altar, the choir (*Open: Mon–Fri 1.30–5pm, Sat 1.30–4pm*) is surrounded by richly carved panels in deep relief. Under the seats, misericords are carved as lion and angel heads.

Return to the ambulatory and continue into the transept.

8 Trivulzio Candelabrum

In the north transept, the 12th-century candelabrum depicts fantastic creatures, the masterpiece of goldsmith

Nicholas of Verdun. Note the pair of copper pulpits that flank the high altar. *Continue along the aisle towards the entrance.*

9 Cappella del Crocifisso

Off the north aisle, and reserved for prayer, is a chapel honouring the crucifix that was carried by San Carlo Borromeo in a 1576 procession praying for deliverance from the plague.

Cross the transept, exiting the north side and turn left.

10 La Salita (ascent to the roof)

A lift (or stairway) ascends to the rooftop, one of Milan's highlights. Here you can wander among the delicate spires and statues and, on clear days, get a breathtaking view of the Alps.

Duomo open: daily 7am–6.45pm. Admission charge. Metro: Duomo.

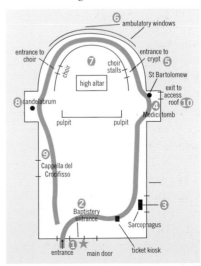

Casa del Manzoni

Behind the highly decorative façade of his eclectic-style home, where he lived from its completion in 1864 until his death (by falling down the steps of neighbouring San Fedele) in 1873, all is just as Manzoni left it, including the study where he wrote much of his work. *Via Morone 1. Tel: (02) 8646 0403. Open: Tue–Fri 9am–noon & 2–6pm. Free admission. Metro: Duomo.*

Cimitero Monumentale

Monumental is the key word in this astonishing final resting place of the once rich and famous. Art Nouveau – called Liberty style here – is at its height in the earlier tombs and monuments, which date from the late 1800s to the mid-20th century. A map, in English, leads to some highlights. The inner circle – Milan's *illuminati* – are buried within the Famae Aedes, and include conductor Arturo Toscanini, poet Salvatore Quasimodo and author Alessandro Manzoni (*see Casa del Manzoni, above*). Many of the monuments are the work of noted Italian sculptors.

I PROMESSI SPOSI

Although not well known outside of the country, Manzoni's work *I Promessi Sposi* (*The Betrothed*) is on the reading list in every Italian school, right up there with Dante. Playing on the theme of love thwarted, Manzoni brought immediacy to his 19th-century Italian readers by weaving in both political and religious themes and characters, conflicts that ring true even today.

Four blocks north of Stazione Porta Garibaldi. Tel: (02) 659 9938. Open: Tue–Fri 8.30am–5.15pm, Sat & Sun 8.30am–5.45pm. Admission charge. Tram: 3, 4.

Civica Galleria d'Arte Moderna

Works of art representing the period from the late 1700s through to the beginnings of modern art are shown in a villa once occupied by Napoleon, at the edge of the public gardens. Highlights are the works of Italian artists and those of the French Impressionists and Post-Impressionists, including Manet, Cézanne and Gauguin. Those who like neoclassical sculpture will admire the works of Canova and others here. *Villa Reale, Via Palestro 16. Tel: (02) 7600 2819. Open: Tue–Sun 9am–5.30pm. Admission charge. Metro: Palestro.*

Civico Museo Archeologico

Opposite the high Baroque Palazzo Arese Litta, the convent of the church of San Maurizio now houses the city's archaeological collections, the highlights of which relate to Roman Milan. The location was not chosen at random, for it sits over portions of the original Roman walls, visible beneath the courtyard, along with a 24-sided Roman tower, **Torre Ansperto**. A model shows what Roman Mediolanum, the original Milan, looked like. The museum also features Greek and Etruscan art and terracotta pieces and ancient Greek ivories from Puglia. It is worth stepping into **San Maurizio** itself (*Open: Tue–Sun 9am–noon & 2–5.30pm*) to see the excellent frescoes by Bernardo Luini and his sons. These almost completely cover the interior, their colours still vibrant after half a millennium.

Corso Magenta 15. Tel: (02) 8645 0011. Open: Tue–Sun 9.30am–5.30pm. Admission charge. Metro: Cadorna.

Milan

Entrance to the archaeology museum at San Maurizio

Milan's architecture

Despite the loss of its buildings to modernisation and war, Milan's architecture covers almost 2,200 years – from Rome's conquest to today's monuments to the gods of commerce. Every major style is encapsulated, adapted and reshaped to reflect Milan's own culture.

Little of Roman Mediolanum remains (*see pp12–13*), but outside San Lorenzo Maggiore, which may have been part of the Roman imperial palace chapel, stand 16 Roman columns from the 2nd and 3rd centuries AD. In the centre is a statue that commemorates the Edict of Milan of 313, which ended the persecution of Christians.

The Edict of Milan proved to be a significant event for Lombard architecture, unleashing a flurry of church building. Roman forms were

Galleria Vittorio Emanuele II

adapted to churches; San Lorenzo, built within decades of the Edict, also incorporates material from other Roman structures.

Sant'Ambrogio, AD 379–86, is another fine example of early Christian architecture. Its interior adapts the massive solidity of the Roman basilica – a long hall ending in an apse and flanked by two columned aisles. The portico and interior also reflect the 11th- and 12th-century Romanesque style popular in the early Middle Ages (*see pp42–3*).

It was from this that the Gothic form developed. New building techniques, especially flying buttresses, allowed for lighter, less massive walls and made large windows possible. Milan's Duomo (*see pp28–9*) is the best example of this exuberant style, with its forest of spires and over 2,000 saints perched

The portico and tower of Sant'Ambrogio

in their niches. The nave, begun in 1385, is pure northern Gothic, one of the few in Italy.

After the Sforza family took over Milan in 1450, they brought in two of the leading Renaissance architects – Antonio Averulino (Il Filarete) and Donato Bramante – who were both greatly influenced by Roman ideals. One of Averulino's first projects was reshaping Castello Sforzesco (*see pp26–7*), and the University of Milan is another Averulino building, its cruciform shape revolutionary and its mix of brick and terracotta brilliant.

Bramante, who began his work in Milan before going to Rome, showed his genius at Santa Maria presso San Satiro (*see p45*), where the façade gives way to a masterpiece of *trompe l'oeil* behind the altar.

As the Renaissance progressed into Mannerism, less attention was paid to classic orders, a trend that culminated in the Baroque, where the straight lines yielded to the curve. In Milan this trend was led by Pellegrino Tibaldi, under the patronage of Cardinals Carlo and Federico Borromeo. The Jesuit church of San Fedele (*see p42*) is an example of his work.

Neoclassicism signalled a return to Roman and Greek forms, advocated in Milan by Giuseppe Piermarini. His Palazzo Reale, built next to the Duomo for the Habsburgs during the Austrian occupation, was rebuilt after serious damage in World War II. He also designed the Teatro alla Scala, similarly rebuilt after bombing.

Like Austria, France occupied Milan before Italy's unification, and the French Second Empire influence shows in the splendid glass-domed Galleria Vittorio Emanuele II (*see p34*). Shortly after, Camillo Boito designed the Cimitero Monumentale (*see p30*), whose eclectic style looked ahead to Art Nouveau. The city continued in this direction with the memorial monuments that are among Milan's finest examples of the style.

A 1902 decorative arts exposition prompted Italian designers to shape Art Nouveau into the uniquely Italian Liberty style. After World War I, European modernism pushed this into Novecento style, particularly favoured by Mussolini and the Fascists. Characterised by clean, flat façades broken by striking relief panels of modernist, stylised heroic figures, a good example is the old tourist office building on Piazza del Duomo.

Novecento decorative panel

Galleria Vittorio Emanuele II

If any one image symbolises Milan, it is this elegantly turned-out shopping mall between Piazza del Duomo and Piazza della Scala. Despite the price tags in its shops and cafés, the Milanese use its grand glass-domed arcades so much that they call it their 'living room'. Built in the middle of the 19th century, it was the largest shopping complex in Europe, and marked the beginning of modern architecture in Italy. Under its 48m (157ft) high dome, the *crème de la crème* of shops sell silverware, high fashion, jewellery and other, more mundane, items. But mostly it is about the cafés, from whose tables half of Milan watches the other half.

Piazza del Duomo. Open: daily 24 hours. Shops open: Mon–Sat 9.30am–1pm & 3.30–7pm. Metro: Duomo.

Giardini Pubblici

Businesslike Milanese don't give up much pavement space for greenery, but, when they do, they do it right. From Piazza Cavour to the line of the former city walls spreads an oasis of lawns, wooded reaches, gardens, pools, fountains, winding paths, playgrounds, a café and a healthy collection of museums. Most of the garden was laid out as parkland in the 1780s, and in 1871 the whole lot, including adjacent villa grounds, was revamped for the World Expo. Inside the gardens are the small **Museo del Cinema** in Palazzo Dugnani (*Tel: (02) 655 4977. Open: Fri–Sun 3–6.30pm. Admission charge*), the **Museo Civico di Storia Naturale** (Natural History Museum) (*Tel: (02) 8846 3280. Open: Tue–Sun 9am–6pm. Free admission*) and the **Planetario**

Piazza della Scala and its famed opera house

Ulrico Hoepli (*Tel: (02) 2953 1181.*
Open for planetarium shows).

La Scala

Fresh from a long period of restoration
that saw the historic backstage areas
enlarged and brought to state-of-the-
art modern standards, La Scala fairly
gleams. The Carrara marble interior
and huge crystal chandeliers have been
restored, the seats have new plush
coverings, the gilding has been touched
up and everything looks as it did when
the great opera house first opened in
1778 (perhaps even better). It is open
for performances, or through the
adjoining Museo La Scala.
Piazza della Scala. Tel: (02) 805 3418.
www.teatroallascala.org. Admission
charge. Metro: Duomo.

Museo La Scala

The only way to see inside the theatre
without attending a performance is via
the museum (and then only if a
performance or rehearsal is not in
progress). The museum contains
enough opera memorabilia to satisfy
the most passionate fan. Highlights are
the costumes worn by the great divas –
Leontyne Price as Aida, Maria Callas as
Anne Boleyn, Renata Tebaldi as Manon
Lescaut. Original designer sketches for
costumes and stage sets, including the
Birnam Wood from *Macbeth*, and the
original deed for the theatre signed by
King Vittorio Emanuele II, join a
touching display of the items on
Verdi's desk at the time of his death.

La Scala. Tel: (02) 8879 2473;
www.teatroallascala.org. Open: daily
9am–12.30pm & 1.30–5.30pm.
Admission charge. Metro: Duomo.

Museo Nazionale della Scienza e della Tecnica Leonardo da Vinci

For those unable to understand the
Italian explanations on the exhibits of
Italy's notable scientific and technical
achievements, the Leonardo da Vinci
Gallery is the place to head. Displayed
here are his drawings and documents
with models, in easy-to-understand
exhibits, which follow the great
inventor's contributions to science.
Maritime enthusiasts will not want to
miss the collection of ship models in
the **Museo Navale**. The museum
surrounds the Renaissance cloister of
the former convent of **San Vittore al
Corpo**, whose adjacent church is one of

Galleria Vittorio Emanuele II was Italy's first
major work of modern architecture

Milan

The Poldi Pezzoli Museum

the most highly decorated churches in the city, with works by several Renaissance artists of the Milanese school. The inlaid choir stalls are from the same period.
Via San Vittore 21. Tel: (02) 485 551; www.museoscienza.org. Open: Tue–Fri 9.30am–4.30pm, Sat & Sun 9.30am–6.50pm. Admission charge. Metro: Sant'Ambrogio.

Museo Poldi Pezzoli

Far more than an art gallery, this private museum was founded by an avid 19th-century collector. Paintings are mixed with collections ranging from Lombard enamels to armour and textiles, all in the context of a furnished period house. Works by Bellini, Botticelli, Mantegna and Tiepolo mix

with displays of Murano glass and Coptic fabrics. Brochures and audio tours are available in English.
Via Manzoni 12. Tel: (02) 794 889. www.museopoldipezzoli.it. Open: Tue–Sun 10am–6pm. Admission charge. Metro: Montenapoleone.

Museo Zucchi

Perhaps the city's quirkiest museum, this one occupies the basement of a shop just off Piazza del Duomo. It displays thousands of hand-printing blocks, some dating from the 1700s, used for applying designs on fabric, a subject close to the heart of Milan's fashion industry. A short video shows the techniques used.
Via Ugo Foscolo 4. Tel: (02) 9025 5230. Open: Mon 3.30–7pm, Tue–Sat 10.30am–7.30pm. Admission charge. Metro: Duomo.

Palazzo Bagatti Valsecchi

A tour here is more akin to visiting the home of a highly cultured and wealthy family than a museum. The two courtyards of this *palazzo* face each other across a street in the middle of the fashion district, both worth investigating, even if you don't stop to tour the museum. Although built in the late 1800s, the *palazzo* was intended to house collections from the 16th century and was designed according to Renaissance aesthetic notions. The emphasis of the museum is on the art of collecting, as well as on the objects themselves. These are nonetheless

impressive, with tapestries, furniture (including children's), rare manuscripts, and paintings by the Renaissance masters. Information on the collections in each room is posted in English. If you would like to savour this house at more leisure, ask to have your ticket stamped for another visit. *Via San Spirito 10. Tel: (02) 7600 6132. www.museobagattivalsecchi.org. Open: Tue–Sun 1–5.45pm. Closed: Aug. Admission charge.*
Metro: Montenapoleone.

Piazza dei Mercanti

In a city with a history of overzealous urban renovation and wartime bombing, it is a pleasant surprise to find this medieval enclave opposite the 16th-century law courts, just off Piazza del Duomo. Built in 1233, the **Palazzo della Ragione** was originally the town hall, the political centre of medieval Milan, and the open arcade beneath it was the market. The black-and-white marble Palazzo degli Osii, built in 1316, forms the other side,

Palazzo Bagatti Valsecchi sits in the centre of the fashion district

overlooking a now quiet square where booksellers often set up shop.

Pinacoteca Ambrosiana

Commissioned by Cardinal Frederico Borromeo to house the valuable collection of documents that it still contains, Pinacoteca Ambrosiana was one of the world's first public libraries when it opened in 1609. The Cardinal's personal art collection was added in 1618, making this an exceptionally rich concentration of arts and letters. On show are paintings by Leonardo da Vinci, Caravaggio and Brueghel, as well as Raphael's cartoons for his Vatican frescoes. Lord Byron is said to have stolen a strand of Lucrezia Borgia's hair from the museum in 1816. The original façade, facing Piazza San Sepolcro, is now the back of the museum.

Piazza Pio XI 2. Tel: (02) 806 921.
www.ambrosiana.eu.
Open: Tue–Sat 10am–5.30pm.
Admission charge. Metro: Duomo.

Pinacoteca di Brera

Milan's largest art museum (not an inconsiderable title in this art-filled city) is a vast complex broken by courtyards. Both the best-known and

An old well is in the centre of one of the Palazzo Bagatti Valsecchi's courtyards

the lesser-known Italian masters are represented, including Caravaggio, Piero della Francesca, Titian, Raphael, Tintoretto, Veronese, Luini, Bramante, Mantegna, Tiepolo and Canaletto. However, there are not only Italian Renaissance paintings; works by Rembrandt, Van Dyck, Braque, Picasso and Modigliani join them. Much of the collection was acquired when the monasteries were closed under Napoleon's rule. The streets surrounding the Pinacoteca are worth exploring for the small galleries, antique stores and Left Bank ambience of its cafés.

Via Brera 28. Tel: (02) 722 631; www.brera.beniculturali.it. Open: Tue–Sat 8.30am–7.30pm, Sun 9am–1pm. Admission charge. Metro: Lanza.

Quadrilatero della Moda (Fashion Quarter)

Although the catwalks of the Fiera di Milano are visible only to those with trade credentials, anyone can enjoy the spectacle of the season's most outrageous – and expensive – fashions simply by strolling along the streets where the designers have their shops. These cluster in the streets south of Piazza Cavour, off Via Monte Napoleone. Among the shop windows of designer boutiques are some lovely old homes and *palazzi*, whose inner courtyards are often visible.

Streets in the area bounded by Via Monte Napoleone, Via della Spiga, Via San Andrea and Via Manzoni. Metro: Monte Napoleone.

San Bernardino alle Ossa

This is perhaps one of Milan's most unsettling churches, where the walls of the Cappella Ossario (Ossuary Chapel) are lined with human bones arranged in patterns. Although this is not an uncommon practice in Iberia, it is seen less often in Italian churches.

Piazza San Stefano. Open: Mon–Fri 7.30am–noon & 2.30–6pm, Sat & Sun 7.30am–noon. Metro: Duomo.

Statue overlooking Piazza dei Mercanti

Walk: Central Milan

While Milan sprawls for a considerable distance, many of its primary sights are relatively close to the Duomo. This route takes you past many of them.

Allow 2 hours, longer with Duomo and museum tours.

Begin at Piazza del Duomo, where the tourist information office can supply maps and current museum and church opening hours, which are good to consult since these change frequently.

1 The Duomo

You can't miss the elaborate exterior, unless it is enclosed in scaffolding (*see pp28–9*).
Leaving the Duomo, walk straight ahead from the left corner of the piazza *onto Via Torino.*

2 Santa Maria presso San Satiro

On the left-hand side of Via Torino, a popular shopping street, is a small opening leading to this surprising Bramante church (*see p45*).
Cross Via Torino and follow Via Spadari to Via Cantù, turning right.

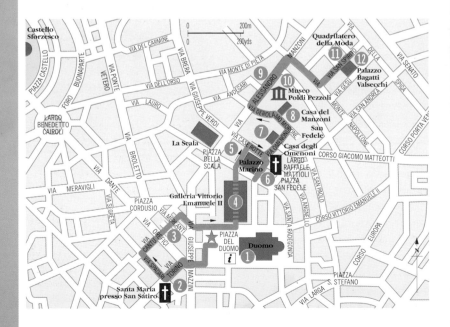

3 Piazza dei Mercanti

Opposite Via Cantù, go through the narrow passage into the centre of medieval Milan (*see pp37–8*). Beyond the arcade is Via Mercanti, under the gaze of St Ambrose, whose statue adorns the old law courts.
Turn right and cross the street, entering the arcaded northern side of the Piazza del Duomo.

4 Galleria Vittorio Emanuele II

To your left is the grand glass-domed gallery (*see p34*).
Walk through to the far end.

5 Piazza della Scala

To your left as you exit the Galleria is La Scala, the world's best-known opera venue (*see p35*). To your right is Palazzo Marino, Milan's city hall.
Leave the piazza at the far side, along Via Case Rotte, circling Palazzo Marino to see its more attractive façade on Piazza San Fedele.

6 San Fedele

The Jesuit church is on the left (*see p42*).
Backtrack a few steps into Largo Raffaele Mattioli and walk straight through to Via Omenoni.

7 Casa degli Omenoni

The street passes under the statues on the façade of the house designed by the sculptor Leone Leoni in 1565.
At the end, turn left.

8 Casa del Manzoni

At the end of the square is the home of the writer Manzoni (*see p30*).
Follow Via Gerolamo Morone beside the Manzoni house, to its end, turning right.

9 Via Alessandro Manzoni

One of Milan's most elegant streets, Via Manzoni is flanked by *palazzi*, whose archways lead into leafy courtyards. Several are open to explore.

10 Museo Poldi Pezzoli

On the right, behind an elegant façade, is this *palazzo*-turned-art-museum (*see p36*). Further on is the Grand Hotel where the composer Giuseppe Verdi died.
Turn right at Via Monte Napoleone.

11 Quadrilatero della Moda

Wander the streets enclosed by Via Monte Napoleone, Via della Spiga, Via San Andrea and Via Manzoni to see the window displays of the great fashion houses (*see p39*).

12 Palazzo Bagatti Valsecchi

Via San Spirito runs between the facing courtyards of this Renaissance-style *palazzo* (*see pp36–7*).
Return to your starting point by Metro from Via Monte Napoleone.

The unusual façade of Casa degli Omenoni

San Fedele

The somewhat severe, highly disciplined Jesuit style of this church is greatly enlivened by Baroque flourishes, showing each at its best. San Fedele is one of Pellegrino Tibaldi's earliest works, and his skill in interpreting the new ideas of the Counter-Reformation made him a favourite of Cardinal Carlo Borromeo, whose hand was in every project of mid-1500s Milan. Baroque and Mannerist (late Renaissance) paintings abound, as does Baroque woodcarving, especially on the confessionals. The carved choir stalls are not original to the church – they were moved here from Santa Maria della Scala when it was torn down to build the opera house.
Piazza San Fedele. Tel: (02) 7200 8027. Open: daily 7.30am–2.30pm & 4–7pm. Metro: Duomo.

The interior of San Sebastiano

San Sebastiano

Five years after designing San Fedele, Tibaldi was chosen by Cardinal Borromeo to design this church in thanksgiving for Milan's deliverance from the plague. The Comerio painting inside the colossal dome is impressive, not so much for its artistic virtuosity as for its size. The round interior still glows with the flickering candles lit in votive offering before the various altars.
Via Torino. Tel: (02) 874 263. Open: Mon–Sat 8.15am–noon & 3–5pm, Sun 9.30am–12.30pm & 3.30–7pm. Metro: Duomo.

San Sepolcro

Dedicated to the Holy Sepulchre in Jerusalem, San Sepolcro sits in the heart of what was once the forum of Roman Milan, or Mediolanum. Reworked in the Counter-Reformation under Cardinal Borromeo and again at the end of the 19th century, there is little left of the Romanesque church except for its long crypt, little changed since the church's construction in 1030. There is a sarcophagus from the 1500s in the apse, with good stone carvings.
Piazza San Sepolcro. Open: Mon–Fri noon–2.30pm, Mass at 12.45pm. Metro: Duomo.

Sant'Ambrogio

The most historic of Milan's many remarkable churches, Sant'Ambrogio was started by Milan's own Saint Ambrose in the 4th century AD, and has led a far from quiet life: in

Carved Romanesque capitals at Sant'Ambrogio

1196 the dome collapsed and was rebuilt, and in 1943 the church was badly damaged by bombing. Additions made through the ages – a monastery (8th century), two bell towers (9th and 12th centuries) the large portico (9th century) and a number of interior embellishments – have made the church a living museum. The atrium, which has excellent carved capitals on its columns, is one of Europe's most important examples of the Romanesque period. From it, a 4th-century portal with stone carvings and 9th-century bronze doors leads inside. Ahead, beneath an outstanding pulpit, is the **Stilicone sarcophagus**, here since the 4th century and surrounded with exceptional deep-relief carvings. The golden altarpiece, inset with stones, was created by master goldsmiths in the time of Charlemagne (after AD 774), and under it is a crypt with the remains of not one, but three saints: Ambrose himself and the two Milanese martyrs for whom he built the church. Through the last chapel on the right is the vibrant mosaic dome of the original 4th-century **Sacello di San Vittore**.

Piazza Sant'Ambrogio 15. Tel: (02) 8645 0895. Open: Mon–Sat 7am–noon & 2–7pm, Sun 7am–1.15pm & 2.30–7.45pm. Treasury: daily 9.30am–noon & 2.30–6pm. Metro: Sant'Ambrogio.

Sant'Eustorgio

The 11th-century church was rebuilt in the following century after being destroyed by Holy Roman Emperor Frederick Barbarossa in his siege of Milan. When Barbarossa left, he took with him the most sacred items of the church's treasury – the relics of the Three Kings. These were returned much later, and are venerated on Epiphany (6 January). The church was rebuilt and renovated so often that it has a little bit of everything, from Romanesque forward, and a little bit of everybody in the local late medieval art world, including Luini and Balduccio, whose marble tomb of Stefano Visconti is an outstanding example of high Gothic.

The church's place in art history, however, is assured by the **Cappella Portinari**, behind the apse – Milan's first real Renaissance ensemble. Commissioned in the 1460s by a Medici banker from Florence as a tomb for himself and St Peter Martyr (humility was never a strong Florentine

Bramante's altar at Santa Maria presso San Satiro

suit), the chapel brings together the work of Balduccio (his reliquary ark for the saint is in the chapel's centre) and Foppa, whose frescoes here are considered his masterpiece. The Foppa fresco cycle shows scenes in the life of St Peter Martyr, with dancing angels around the base of the dome.
Piazza Sant'Eustorgio. Tel: (02) 5810 1583. Church open: daily 7.45am–noon & 3.30–6.15pm. Chapel open: Tue–Sun 10am–6pm (July–Aug 4–6.30pm). Admission charge to chapel. Tram: 3.

Santa Maria della Grazie

Bramante gave this 15th-century Gothic church its Renaissance appearance by rebuilding the sanctuary and apse and adding the charming 'Frog Cloister'. Inside, in the second chapel on the right, a Caravaggio painting stands in for the Titian stolen by Napoleon's army in 1797 and taken off to the Louvre, where it remains.

In the adjoining **Cenacolo Vinciano** is one of the most widely recognised of all paintings, Leonardo da Vinci's *The Last Supper*. Painted during 1496–7, on a dry surface that began to deteriorate almost immediately, the work captures the moment of shock and disbelief as Christ announces that one of his disciples will betray him. The work's power is intensified by the use of a stable base that allowed Leonardo more time to concentrate on details of facial expression, difficult in the volatile fresco medium. Generally regarded as one of the great masterpieces of

Western art, the painting shows the ravages of time despite some recent restoration.

Piazza Santa Maria della Grazie.
Tel: (02) 8942 1146. Church open: daily 7am–noon & 3–7pm, Cenacolo Tue–Sun 8.15am–6.45pm. Admission charge. Cenacolo tickets are timed, and must be reserved well in advance; operators speak English. Metro: Conciliazione.

Santa Maria presso San Satiro

It is best to enter this church before reading about it, admiring the deep-vaulted sanctuary from the entrance before walking closer to realise that its depth is a very skilfully designed illusion. Lacking the space for a grand apse behind the altar, Bramante created, in less than a metre (3ft), the optical illusion of a sanctuary worthy of a cathedral. The Cappella della Pietà, to the left, has some early medieval frescoes.

Via Torino 9. Tel: (02) 7202 1804.
Open: Mon–Sat 8.30–11.30am & 3.30–5.30pm, Sun 9.30–10.30am & 4.30–5.30pm. Metro: Duomo.

Milan

The church of Santa Maria della Grazie

Train and boat tour: Lake Como from Milan

Milan is so close to the town of Como, the gateway to Lake Como, that it is easy to take a day's excursion there using public transport. Seamless boat–train connections make it even more convenient. Funiculars into the mountains give a new perspective to the Alpine backdrops, as well as adding a third means of transport to an outing.

Allow a full day. Rise early to fit everything in.

Trains from Milan's Stazione Nord arrive at Como's Stazione Milano Nord, near the ferry dock. Hydrofoils and slower boats ply the lake on a regular schedule, more frequently in summer when most major towns are connected twice an hour. Note that some services slow to a halt during the *mezzogiorno* – the two hours at midday when many attractions are also closed. Savvy travellers plan to join locals by eating lunch then, and strolling in parks and promenades.
Navigazione Lago di Como, Piazza Cavour. Tel: (031) 579 211; www.navigazionelaghi.it

1 Milan
Depart Milan's Stazione Nord for Como's Milano Nord station. On arrival, cross the street to the lake promenade and turn left to reach the boat landing to board a fast hydrofoil or a slower steamer for Bellagio.

2 Bellagio
From the dock, a short walk along the lake to the right leads to the gardens at **Villa Melzi d'Eril** (*see p81*). To the left along the lake front, there are numerous cafés and restaurants that serve lunch, and the streets behind are filled with shops and galleries worth visiting. *Return to Como at leisure.*

3 Como
From the landing, it is a short walk through Piazza Cavour to the **Duomo** (*see pp78–9*). The promenade along the lake shore, to the right, leads through public gardens and along the marina.

4 Brunate
Alternatively, head directly to the funicular by walking left along the lake from the dock. Rising precipitously to the mountain-top village of **Brunate**, the funicular has been making this 1,000m (3,280ft) climb since 1894. Over dinner or an aperitif in a terrace café at the top, you can watch the sun

set and the lights come on around the lake and in Como, directly below. *Funicolare Brunate, Piazza de Gasperi. Tel: (031) 303 608. Open: daily*

6am–10.30pm. Admission charge. Return to Piazza de Gasperi via the funicular and walk along the lake to the train station for the return ride to Milan.

Como's marina, with the mountain-top village of Brunate above

Train and boat tour: Lake Como from Milan

Excursion: Monza

As the seat of Lombardy's government under Queen Teodolinda in the 6th century AD and Frederick Barbarossa in the 12th, and later as a country retreat for the Habsburg rulers of Milan during the Austrian years, Monza has a royal lineage. There is no mistaking its Villa Reale for anything but a royal palace, and the cathedral is filled with reminders of its patron queen.

Many travellers follow the royal lead, staying here to avoid both Milan's hotel prices and the high-voltage buzz of its streets. After a day in Milan, the gentle rhythms of Monza's pedestrianised central *piazze* (squares) are pleasant indeed. Alternatively, Monza makes an easy half-day trip; trains to and from Milan's Centrale and Garibaldi railway stations stop here at least every 30 minutes, and it's a 15-minute ride.

Via Italia leads from Largo Mazzini, near the railway station, through the old town centre, which retains some of its medieval appearance. This pedestrianised street passes Piazza del Duomo, then leads to the 13th-century **Arengario**, an outstanding example of a medieval city hall with an arcaded market at street level. Via Carlo Alberto continues north past antique shops, leading to a wooded park, the **Boschetti**. Beyond, at the southern end of the Parco di Monza, begin the grounds of Villa Reale.

Ufficio Informazioni Turistiche, Piazza Carducci. Tel: (039) 323 222. Open: Mon–Fri 9am–noon & 3–6pm, Sat 9am–noon.

Duomo

The best time to see the Duomo is in the late afternoon, when the stonework, pinnacles and rose window of the splendid west-facing façade catch the golden glow of the setting sun. The interior is just as arresting, with elaborate *tromp l'oeil* in its vaulting. To the left of the sanctuary, the **Cappella di Teodolinda** holds the 5th-century **Corona Ferrea**, said to contain a nail from Christ's Cross, and which crowned the kings of Italy from medieval times through to Napoleon. Teodolinda's tomb is in the sanctuary, and scenes of her life decorate the walls of the chapel. Some of her gifts to the church, as well as her small crown, are in the **Museo Serpero**, off a small cloister reached from the nave. *www.duomomonza.it.*

*Duomo open: daily 9am–noon &
3–6.30pm. Museo open: Tue–Sat
9–11.30am & 3–5.30pm, Sun
10.30am–noon & 3–5.45pm. Cappella di
Teodolinda open: Tue–Sat 9–11.30am &
3–5.30pm, Sun 11.30am–noon &
3–5.45pm. Admission charge.*

Palazzo Reale

The Austrian archduke decamped here
from Milan to escape the summer heat,
and his palace spreads grandly at the
southern end of the Parco di Monza. In
front is the **Roseto Niso Fumagalli**, a
formal hedged rose garden and pools.

*Viale Regina Margherita di Savoia.
Garden open: Mon–Fri 8.30am–noon
& 2–5pm, longer hours during summer,
closed Aug.*

Parco di Monza

Walking and bicycle trails weave their
way through the wooded park and
alongside the river, passing villas, tent
pitches, cafés, old mills, a golf course
and the **Autodromo** of Formula One
racing fame. Bike rentals can be found
at the southern end of the park, close to
the Porta Monza.

Open: daily 7.30am–dusk.

Monza's Duomo

Driving tour: Valle d'Aosta

The valley carved by the Dora Baltea River attracts skiers and hikers today, but in earlier times there were trade caravans and Roman legions here. Although distances are short, so much breathtaking scenery tempts travellers to linger that this excursion could easily take several days.

Follow the A-4 west from Milan to the A-4–A-5, then go north on the A-5 to St Vincent. Turn north onto the R-46, signposted 'Breuil-Cervenia'.

Allow 1 day, more if you plan to go skiing or walking.

1 Lago Bleu and Monte Cervino (the Matterhorn)

The scenic high point is not **Breuil-Cervenia**, the ugly jumble of bunker-like hotels where cable cars begin climbing the mountain, but the magical foreground of Lago Bleu a few kilometres before the town. This crystal Alpine tarn reflects the Matterhorn in a picture-perfect scene, framed in dark larch trees.
Retrace your route back down the R-46, then follow S-26 west.

2 Castello di Fénis

From 13th-century origins, the castle's highlight is a charming 15th-century courtyard with a curved stairway and wooden balconies. The castle and chapel are covered in frescoes.
Tel: (0165) 764 263; www.aostavalley. com. Open: mid-Mar–June & Sept 9am–6.30pm; July & Aug 9am–7.30pm; Oct–Feb 10am–noon & 1.30–4.30pm. Closed: Tue, Sun & hols 10am–noon & 1–5.30pm. Admission charge.

Continue west on S-26 to Aosta.

3 Aosta

Significant parts of a Roman-built town remain, including the well-preserved **Teatro Romano**, the **Arch of Augustus** (25 BC) and walls (*see pp12–13*). The **Museo Archaeologico** has outstanding local finds.
Piazza Roncas 5. Tel: (0165) 33 352; www.regione.vda.it. Open: daily 10am–12.30pm & 2.30–6pm. Admission charge.

The ecclesiastical complex of **Sant'Orso** packs centuries of art into its church, bell tower, crypts and cloister.
Tel: (0165) 262 026. Open: daily 8am–7pm. Free admission. Turismo, Piazza Chanoux 8. Tel: (0165) 33 352. Open: daily 10am–12.30pm & 2.30–6pm.

Five kilometres (3 miles) west, in the wine-growing village of Sarre, **Castello Reale** was the 'hunting lodge' of Italian King Umberto I. Tours begin hourly.
Tel: (0165) 257 539; www.regione.vda.it.

Open: Mar–June & Sept 9am–6.30pm;
July & Aug 9am–7.30pm; Oct–Feb
Tue–Sat 10am–noon & 1.30–4.30pm,
Sun & hols 10am–noon &
1.30–5.30pm.

At Sarre, cross the valley, following R-47
south, signposted 'Cogne'.

4 Gran Paradiso and Cogne

Parco Nazionale del Gran Paradiso is
a wilderness of valleys and peaks. **Cogne**,
one of its few villages, is backed by
mountains. Beyond, **Cascata di Lillaz**
drops in several long waterfalls.
Informazione Turistiche, Castello di Sarre.
Tel: (0165) 257 854; www.granparadiso.
net. Open: July–Aug daily 10am–12.30pm
& 2.30–6pm; Sept–June Fri–Sun & hols
10am–12.30pm & 2.30–5pm.

Closed: Christmas Day, Boxing Day, New
Year's Day.

Retrace R-47 to S-26, heading west.

5 Monte Bianco (Mont Blanc)

Monte Bianco appears ahead at the end
of the valley. The chic mountain resort of
Courmayeur has other imposing peaks
to provide an Alpine backdrop for its
designer boutiques. The **Museo Alpino**
features displays on early explorations of
the mountains.
Piazza Henry 2. Tel: (0165) 842 357.
Open: Tue–Sun 9.30am–6.30pm.
Admission charge.

From **Entreves** beyond, aerial rides
lift up to Monte Bianco's ridge line.
APT, Piazzale Monte Bianco 13. Tel: (0165)
842 060. Open: 9am–noon & 3–6pm.

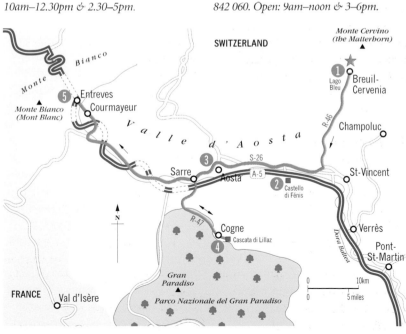

Lago Maggiore

Despite its name, Lago Maggiore, which means 'major lake', this is Italy's second largest at 65km (40 miles) long and 4km (2½ miles) across at its widest. However, it makes up for its secondary status with knock-out good looks. Mountains surround it on all sides, sometimes dropping almost straight into its waters and elsewhere leaving a gently sloping shoreline.

The Swiss–Italian border crosses the upper reaches of Lake Maggiore, so a day trip around the lake becomes an international expedition, even if border formalities are most often a pleasant wave through. The Italians share the lake with the Swiss, and it is a popular weekend destination for the latter; many attractions accept Swiss francs as well as euros.

Steamers, hydrofoils (*corse rapide*) and car ferries (*traghetti*) connect the shore towns with a frequent service, and roads circle it, rarely out of sight of the water. Towns on the southwestern shore are connected to Milan by train, while Laveno and northern points on the eastern shore are on rail lines from Garibaldi and Cadorna stations.

Cable cars of every variety carry passengers from lakeside points to the mountains around the lake for long-distance mountain views and a different perspective on the shore and lake.
Distretto Turistico, Piazza Marconi 16. Tel: (0323) 301 50; www.distrettolaghi.it.

Open: Mar–Oct daily 10am–12.30pm & 3–6.30pm; Nov–Feb Mon–Fri 10am–12.30pm & 3–6.30pm. Navigazione Lago Maggiore. Tel: (800) 551 801; www.navigazionelaghi.it

Angera

Most visitors come to the lake's southeastern corner to see the castle – and rightly so. Yet they may leave too soon, without enjoying the rest of the peninsula it occupies.

Museo dei Trasporti

This open-air hotchpotch of hundreds of land conveyances, from Prince Alberto's 1797 phaeton to the original 1894 Brunate funicular, is possibly the most endearing and captivating museum in northern Italy. Arranged in a maze of passageways that resemble railway platforms, vehicles and related artefacts are so abundant that visitors need to look in all directions for fear of missing a horse-drawn ambulance or Pope Pius IX's railway-carriage chapel.

Follow tracks into a coal mine or descend the escalator into a subway station; museums don't get any quirkier, less high-tech – or more fun.
Off S-629, Ranco. Tel: (0331) 976 614. Open: Tue–Sun 10am–noon & 2–6pm. Admission charge.

Rocca Borromeo

Guarding the southern end of Lake Maggiore since the 13th century, the castle once faced a sister fortress at Arona, and between them the castles controlled access to the lake. The original medieval defensive structure remains intact, with later additions by the Visconti, from whom the Borromeos (*see pp60–61*) purchased it in the mid-1400s. This progression, made without destroying the original medieval construction, makes Rocca Borromeo worth visiting. A 14th-century fresco cycle in the Sala di Giustizia depicts the battle in which the

Ranco's Museo dei Trasporti is filled with early vehicles

Visconti won the castle. These are considered some of the finest examples of non-sacred medieval frescoes to have survived, painted by masters at the apex of the style.

Inside the castle, along with an outstanding collection of mechanical toys, the **Museo della Bambola** displays more than 1,000 dolls, and a separate building houses fashions worn by overprivileged (and probably uncomfortable) children since the 1800s.
Via alla Rocca. Tel: (0331) 931 300; www.roccaborromeo.it. Castle and Museo della Bambola open: daily mid-Mar–mid-Oct 9am–5.30pm. Admission charge.

Southern Maggiore

The most heavily visited part of the lake is this southern section, which is most easily reached by train from

Hikers enjoy the trails of the Fondotoce nature reserve

Milan and from nearby Malpensa airport. In this area you will also find a thicker concentration of hotels.

Arona

Arona is a good base for those arriving by train, since it is well supplied with accommodation and restaurants, and has good access to the various types of transport around the lake.
Turismo, Piazzale Duca d'Aosta.
Tel: (0322) 243 601.

Arona's claim to fame – and you really should see it – is the 23.5m (75ft) tall statue of **San Carlo Borromeo**, cast in bronze and copper in 1698. One of the world's tallest statues, it commemorates the local boy who made good by becoming an abbot at age 12, and a cardinal and Archbishop of Milan at 22. (A little family money and influence didn't hurt, but he was

undeniably a talented cleric.) Inside the statue, 145 stairs lead to the 2.4m (8ft) head, from which you can survey the world through one eye.
Signposted from S-33, north of town.
Open: daily Apr–Sept 9.15am–12.30pm
& 2–6.30pm; weekends only Oct & Mar.

Fondotoce

The wide Golfo Borromeo separates Stresa from Verbania, ending inland in the relatively undeveloped wetlands of the **Riserva Naturale di Fondotoce**, a reed-filled bird habitat on the delta of the River Toce. Walking and bike trails crisscross the area, and there are tent pitches inside the reserve. You can book guided walks and motorboat cruises with park naturalists at the office.
Via Canale 48, Verbania Fondotoce.
Tel: (0322) 240 239. Office open Mon–
Fri 9am–noon & 2–5pm, Sat 9am–noon.

Stresa

Less changed by the vagaries of 21st-century economies than many other lake resorts, Stresa's impressive row of grand hotels still sparkle as they did in the Belle Époque. The streets are lined with expensive shops, frequented by people who can afford to buy. Ernest Hemingway chose one of its luxury hotels, the Grand Hotel des Îles Borromées, as a setting in *A Farewell to Arms*.

Ufficio Turistico, Piazza Marconi 16. Tel: (0323) 301 150.

From Piazzale Lido, north of the centre of town, a cable car gives passengers a chance to look down at the hotels and the Borromean Islands as they ride to **Monte Mottarone**'s summit. Lakes Maggiore and Orta, the Alps and even Milan are visible from the top.

Funivia il Mottarone. Tel: (0323) 303 99; www.terradeilaghi.com. Open: daily 9.30am–5.20pm. Admission charge.

From a stop halfway up the cable-car ride, it is a short walk to the **Giardino Botanico Alpinia** (Alpine Garden), where 800 varieties of Alpine plants have been gathered from mountainous regions of the world. Labelled by name and origin, they fill beds that cover a hilltop. From the summer house there are striking views of the lake and islands.

Alpino. Tel: (0323) 302 95; www.giardinoalpinia.it. Open: Apr–Oct 9.30am–6pm. Admission charge.

Just south of Stresa, **Villa Pallavicino** has filled its park with exotic animals and birds. The formal gardens are impressive as well, planted in solid beds of colour.

Via Sempione Sud 8 (Verbania). Tel: (800) 248 039; www.parcozoopallavicino.it. Open: daily Mar–Oct 9am–6pm. Admission charge.

A paraglider's eye view from the summit of Monte Mottarone

Boat tour: Borromean Islands

Whether the first view of the islands in the Golfo Borromeo is from the shore, from the hills above or from a boat, the palaces, terraced gardens and jumble of stucco buildings are sights that no visitor can – or should – resist.

Unless you make an early start, the schedules of the regular lake steamer make it difficult to visit all three islands in one day without feeling as though you are running a marathon. If time presses, spend more on a day ticket from one of the taxi services, which allows you to move freely and promptly, even at midday when the steamers do not stop at Isola Madre. Look for the *biglietteria* (ticket office) next to Stresa's steamer landing.
Navigazione Lago Maggiore. Tel: (800) 551 801 (freephone); www.navigazionelaghi.it

From the top of the Isola Bella gardens

1 Isola Madre gardens
Almost the entire island is planted with trees, and swathes of lawn are ornamented by flower beds. The woodland walks that skirt the perimeter are open to lake views, and the entire southern shore is a terraced promenade, its vines so neatly clipped against the wall that they appear to be a hedge. Circle back up the wide walkway to the villa and admire Europe's largest Kashmir cypress tree.
Tel: (0323) 312 61; www.borromeoturismo.it. Open Apr–Oct 9am–5.30pm. Admission charge.

2 Villa
Signs in four languages identify art and furnishings in each room of this 16th-century manor house. While these are impressive, the house's highlights are room-sized puppet theatres and displays of marionettes and scenery.
Admission included in the entry fee for the gardens.

3 Isola Bella: Palazzo Borromeo

From the boat landing, walk left along the shore. Stop first in the chapel, opposite the entrance, to see the carved marble tombs, considered the finest examples of Renaissance funerary art in Lombardy. The building of the high-Baroque ancestral home of the Borromeos (still owned by the family) began in 1670, but the impressive three-storey Salon was completed only in 1948. Most astonishing is the gold and stucco Throne Room with its giant Mannerist caryatids supporting the cornice.

Tel: (0323) 305 56; www.borromeoturismo.it. Open: Apr–Sept 9am–noon & 1.30–5.30pm; Oct 9am–5pm. Admission charge.

4 Isola Bella gardens

From atop the hulking and fussy wall of the Teatro Massimo (Massimo Theatre), the views down onto both sides of the Isola Bella gardens are spectacular. Patterned flower beds fall in terraces framed by sculpted evergreens. The statuary and stone flourishes make this a triumph of Italianate garden style.

Admission included in the entry fee for the palace.

5 Streets

Take time to wander in the narrow passageways leading to the shore. Classy boutiques mingle with kitschy souvenir stalls, and flowering vines run amok on the walls. The lake shore is lined with cafés and eateries.

6 Isola Pescatore

After touring the islands' sights, it is refreshing simply to wander in the stone streets and linger in the cafés of this more workaday (but equally picturesque) island, where a few fishermen still ply their trade on the lake. You can understand why Hemingway liked it here.

Isola Pescatore floats beneath the Alps on Lake Maggiore

Boat tour: Borromean Islands

Central Lake Maggiore

Mountains border both shores, and recede layer after layer in the northward vistas. Some of the best views up the lake – and of the shore towns – are from the lake steamers, and even from the car ferry that crosses from Intra (part of Verbania) to Laveno.
Turismo, Corso Zanitello 6/8, Pallanza (Verbania). Tel: (0323) 503 249; fax: (0323) 507 722.

Cannero Riviera

On a lake lined with attractive waterfront promenades, it is hard to find a more pleasant one to stroll along than Cannero's. Here there are frequent cafés overlooking the water, and a small fortified island. Hire a water taxi to see the island's castle up close.
Tel (mobile): 339 834 3322; www.sanobanano.it

Cannobio

Almost on the Swiss border, Cannobio is a busy little town with the curious Renaissance **Santuario della Pietà**, housing a small parchment picture with a number of miracles attributed to it. The church is right by the boat landing.
Open: 7.30am–noon & 2–7pm.

Follow brown '**Val Cannobina**' signs inland from the southern end of town to reach a deep, mysterious gorge spanned by an arched stone bridge. For views from water level, take the stone path opposite the **Oratorio Sant'Anna**, which stands at the bridge. The scenic valley beyond is worth exploring if narrow mountain roads don't worry you.

Laveno

It is easy to overlook this pretty waterfront in the rush to catch the car ferry, which shortens driving distances by shuttling cars across to Intra.
Navigazione Lago Maggiore. Tel: (800) 551 801 (freephone); www.navigazionelaghi.it

A funny little bucket-like gondola lifts passengers to the summit of **Sasso del Ferro** for the stunning views. One of the lake's most photographed sights is south of the town – the lovely 13th-century hermitage **L'Eremo di Santa Caterina del Sasso Ballaro**, built into a cliff face between the villages of Cerro and Reno. Steep stone steps lead down to it.
Open: daily Apr–Oct 9am–noon & 2.30–6pm, Nov–Feb Sat & Sun 9am–noon & 2–6pm. Free admission.

The harbour at Calde

Oratorio Sant'Anna sits atop a deep gorge

North along the shore, the charming little harbour of **Calde** hides beneath a rock promontory. Find it by following signs to its well-known restaurant, La Vela.

Luino

Known chiefly for the giant Wednesday market on Piazza Garibaldi (don't even think of driving there on market day), this eastern shore town centres on a very attractive marina filled with colourful boats, which bob under the protection of a golden Madonna. The elaborate 17th-century **Oratorio dei SS Giuseppe e Dionigi** overlooks Piazza Garibaldi.

Villa Taranto

Snuggled into Verbania's protected shore, the gardens of Villa Taranto were the passion of a retired Scottish army officer and botanist for three decades. In a land of primarily (and not surprisingly) Italianate-style gardens, the more relaxed and flowing lines of an English garden park are a pleasant contrast. Its formal elements – the stunning terraced garden and the avenue from the cherub fountain to the mausoleum – are set in a park filled with thousands of exotic and native trees and shrubs. More than 20,000 plant varieties, from climates as distant as the Amazonian rainforest, thrive here within sight of the pre-Alps.

Pallanza. Tel: (0323) 556 667; www.villataranto.it. Open: Apr–Oct daily 8.30am–6.30pm. Admission charge.

The Borromeo family

Generation after generation, the Borromeos have influenced art, architecture, religion and politics. Driven from Florence in 1370 after playing lead parts in a revolt, the Borromeos arrived in Milan and immediately became active members of the community.

The first of the great Lombard Borromeos was Vitaliano I, born in 1391, who became treasurer for the Duke of Milan in 1418. Selling the duke supplies, Vitaliano quickly acquired money to buy the castle at Arona and land at Cannobio, Mergozzo, Vogogna and Val Vigezzo.

When the duke's son-in-law, Francesco Sforza, inherited the

The huge statue of San Carlo Borromeo at Ancona

dukedom, Vitaliano supported Sforza's rule in Milan. His son, Giovanni III, managed to solve the duchy's financial woes when Sforza died in 1466 and, in gratitude, was granted more land around Lake Maggiore. Under his leadership, the family holdings became strong enough to be called the 'Borromeo State'. Giovanni became a major patron of artists and sculptors, commissioning important works.

When the conflict between the Sforzas, the Swiss, the French and the Holy Roman Empire reduced the family's influence, the Borromeos wisely withdrew to their lake territories under the leadership of Gilberto I, and worked at developing their control of the lake and its commerce. All the while, they were building Renaissance residences on the islands off Stresa, now called the Borromean Islands.

Gilberto's son, Gilberto II, married Margherita Medici, sister of Pope Pius IV (Gian Angelo Medici). Their son Carlo, born 1538, entered the Church and quickly rose in its hierarchy in Rome. When his uncle appointed him cardinal in 1560 (at age 22) he also appointed him Archbishop of Milan.

The Borromeo palace on Isola Bella

Returning there, Carlo established the first seminaries, reformed the Church's administration, established synods, and began pastoral visits to his churches in response to the Protestant Reformation. Carlo's younger cousin Federico also entered the Church and rose quickly to the rank of cardinal as well, succeeding Carlo as Archbishop of Milan at his death. It was Federico's zeal that led to Carlo being proclaimed St Carlo Borromeo in 1610.

The Cardinals Borromeo retained the family interest in art. Federico established a special committee to reconstruct and restore churches, and established the Biblioteca Ambrosiana, to which he bequeathed his personal art collection. He also erected a monumental bronze statue of his sainted cousin at the family seat of Arona (*see p54*).

In the mid-17th century, the family's aristocratic stature was enhanced when Carlos III's son, Renato III, married Giulia Arese, becoming the first Borromeo-Arese. A second son became a cardinal and papal legate, and the third, Vitaliano VI, was a military officer and diplomat representing Spain. A member of the Milan Council of State, Vitaliano VI was also a major benefactor of the arts and began the greatest development of the palace on Isola Bella.

His successor, Carlos IV, also followed a military and political career, serving as Viceroy of Naples and in other diplomatic roles that brought the family even wider prestige. Gilberto V successfully guided the family fortunes through the vicissitudes of the 18th-century French and Austrian occupations, as he continued construction on Isola Bella and began serious art collections for it.

With the unification of Italy in the 1860s, the family's political power began to diminish. However, the family still retains its long commitment to the arts, preserving the vast Borromeo collections and properties, and administering them through a trust for public benefit.

Northern Maggiore

Boats travel frequently from the southern part of the lake to Locarno; even more leave from Luino. A hydrofoil departs from Arona at 9.30am and delivers passengers to Locarno before lunch, making this a pleasant and scenic day trip. Boat traffic is less frequent at this end of the lake, and so it is usually easier to visit the smaller towns by bus (*No 21*) from Locarno, or to drive across the border. The crossing usually involves few delays – if any at all. In either case, you will need a passport, since Switzerland is not a member of the EU.

Ente Turistico Lago Maggiore. Tel: (091) 791 0091; www.maggiore.ch
When calling Switzerland, use country code 0041 or +41.

Ascona

Picture a pretty little Italian lakeside town in the hands of a team of Swiss housekeepers, and you have Ascona. It looks very Italian, but it's far too neat and tidy. It is a lovely blend of the two nations, with window boxes overflowing with red geraniums. There's not a whole lot to do here except shop in the upmarket (and expensive) boutiques, but it's pleasant just sitting at a café along the Lungolago and enjoying the scene. Or go in the autumn for the Settimane Musicali's classical performances.

Ente Turistico, Casa Serodine. Tel: (091) 785 1965; www.settimane-musicali.ch

Gondola ascending Sasso del Ferro

Bellinzona

Castles are almost commonplace in this historical crossroads of trans-Alpine trade routes, and three overlook the town. The oldest, and most atmospheric, is the 13th-century **Castello di Montebello**, reached by passageways and stone stairs from Piazza Collegiata (a short walk from the railway station). Inside, along with battlements to walk around, is an archaeology museum.

Tel: (0541) 675 180.
Open: daily mid-Mar–Oct 10am–6pm. Admission charge.

Brissago

Caught in the narrow space between mountain and lake, Brissago makes the most of its space with a kilometre (0.6-mile) long promenade, the **Lungolago**, bordered by subtropical trees. Plants from even warmer climates grow unprotected by glasshouses on the nearby island, **Isole Brissago**, which lake waters keep at above freezing temperatures year-round. The botanical garden, created in 1885 by a Russian baroness, is divided into areas corresponding with the continents where the plants are native. Medicinal plants, some extinct in their natural habitat, surround a neo-Roman bath. *Tel: (091) 791 4361; www.isolebrissago.ch. Open: daily Apr–Oct 9am–5pm. Admission charge.*

Some lake steamers stop at the island, and there is a more frequent service from Porto Ronco, 2km (1¼ miles) north of Brissago.

Locarno

The odd curving shape of Locarno's central **Piazza Grande** has an interesting story. The curving row of arcaded buildings follows the original building line, from when the houses rose directly from the lake. Lower water levels left the area high and dry, and it was paved with river stones to form the *piazza*. Behind its buildings rises an area of twisted narrow streets, arcades and garden-filled courtyards. Step through the archways to see medieval houses, fountains and lush gardens, especially in Piazzetta de' Capitani, Piazzetta delle Corporazione, Casa del Negromante and Casa dei Canonici, which has a medieval garden.

Near the railway station, a *funicolare* (funicular railway) carries passengers to **Orselina** for views and access to a *funivia* (cable car) bound for even higher **Cardada**. Locarno is the starting point for the scenic Centovalli train excursion (*see pp74–5*).

Castello di Montebello lies in beautiful surroundings

Excursion: Lake Varese

Overshadowed by larger lakes, Lake Varese and the region that surrounds it are rich in fascinating sights but little known to foreign tourists. A medieval mountain-top town enlivened by modern frescoes, a 5th-century archaeological site, a holy mountain and the quiet, reedy lake shore with its birdlife and nature reserve all await the curious traveller. The attractive old town of Azzate makes a good centre from which to explore the region (see p177).

Arcumeggia

The narrow road to Arcumeggia winds upwards alarmingly to reach a cluster of medieval stone buildings and roughly cobbled passageways. Not at all the 'murals for tourists' one would expect, these mid-20th-century paintings are small, their colours subdued and their subjects diverse, ranging from religious themes to a bicycle race. No boutiques or souvenir shops mar the scene, and only two eating places await visitors.

Follow S-394 from Laveno to Cittiglio, turning left to Casalzuigno, from which the Arcumeggia road branches to the left.

At the turning in Casalzuigno, **Villa della Porta Bozzolo** stands in a splendid Baroque garden set around a wide terraced staircase with stone balustrades and statuary. The original 1500s farmhouse was transformed into a grand villa with the addition of 18th-century frescoes and rococo interior details.

Tel: (0332) 624 136;

Palazzo Estense from the gardens

Fresco at Arcumeggia

www.fondoambiente.it. Open: Mar–Sept Tue–Sun 10am–6pm; Oct–mid-Dec & Feb Tue–Sun 10am–5pm. Admission charge.

Castel Seprio

The walls and foundations of a 5th-century basilica, and portions of even earlier stone towers and houses, show a village destroyed in 1285, when Milan and Turin fought for control of the region. An excellent free booklet in English maps and describes the village, through which visitors can walk, although it is an active archaeological sight. Also at the site is the 8th-century church of **Santa Maria Foris Portas**, with Byzantine frescoes.
Via Castelvecchio. Tel: (0331) 820 438. Open: Feb–Oct Tue–Sat 8.30am–7.30pm, Sun 9.30am–7pm (closes earlier Nov–Jan). Admission charge.

Castiglione Olona

This rather ordinary town has a most surprising corner tucked into a ravine at one side. Looking more Tuscan than Lombardian, the enclave was the work of a local cardinal who spent much of his life in Florence as a papal legate. Returning to Lombardy, he began reshaping his village by reworking his family villa, **Palazzo Branda Castiglioni** (*Piazza Garibaldi. Tel: (0331) 858 903. Open: Apr–Sept Tue–Sat 9am–noon & 3–6pm, Sun 10.30am–12.30pm & 3–6pm; Oct–Mar Tue–Sat 9am–noon & 3–6pm, Sun 3–6pm. Admission charge*). The **Collegiata** church at the top of the hill has outstanding Renaissance frescoes in the baptistery, but the artistic ideas of the time are unfettered in the **Chiesa di Villa**, opposite the *palazzo* (*Open: Tue–Sun 10am–noon & 2.30–7pm. Admission charge*).

Varese

Parks and terraced formal gardens surround the richly decorated former villa of the d'Este family, **Palazzo Estense**, built in the 1700s and which Stendhal called 'Versailles in Milan' (*Via Sacco. Open: Mon–Sat 10am–noon & 2–6.30pm*). In **Campo dei Fiori** park, north of the town, is **Sacro Monte di Varese**, an ascending series of 17th-century chapels with larger-than-life figures depicting biblical scenes.
IAT Tourist Information Office, Via Carrobbio 2. Tel: (0332) 283 604; www.vareselandoftourism.it

Lago d'Orta

Wooded hillsides embrace exclusive little Lake Orta, only 13km (8 miles) long and barely 2km (1¼ miles) at its widest. The road around this most enchanting and romantic of lakes is 33km (21 miles) long. What it lacks in size it makes up for in beauty, with a medieval town at its centre and a little island of garden villas just offshore. It's enough to make even the most dedicated non-photographer wish for a camera.

Transportation between lake towns and to the island is provided by **Navigazione Lago d'Orta** (*Tel: (0322)* 844 862. *Operates daily Easter–mid-Oct, mid-Oct–Nov Sat & Sun*) and **Servizio Pubblico Motoscafi Lago d'Orta**

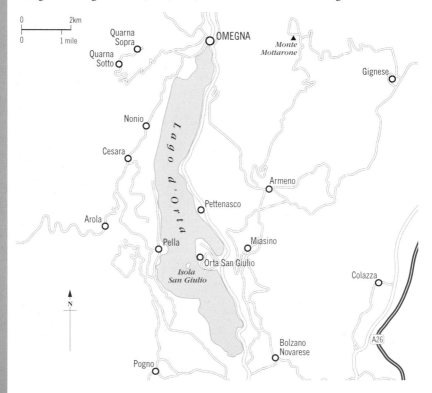

Lago d'Orta

(Piazza Motta, Orta San Giulio. Tel: (333) 605 0288; www.motoscafipubbliciorta.it).

Isola San Giulio

The centrepiece of the tiny island is its excellent Romanesque **Basilica di San Giulio**, founded in the 4th century and rebuilt in the 9th and 10th. Stone-carved reliefs and columns date from this era, and the campanile was added in the 12th century. Inside is a 12th-century pulpit of Oira marble, carved in animal

designs. *Tel: (032) 290 358. Open: daily in summer, Tue–Sun in winter.*

Legend holds that the church was founded by San Giulio, who drove away the snakes to make the island habitable. In the crypt is his sarcophagus. **Via del Silenzio** leads around the moody little island, with glimpses into gardens.

Omegna

By comparison to well-heeled medieval Orta San Giulio (*see pp68–9*), Omegna

Isola San Giulio is in the lake near Orta San Giulio

is the plain-Jane cousin. However, it is not without charm, sitting at the outlet of the lake against a soaring mountainside. Flower boxes line the riverside and bridge, and a Thursday market fills the tree-shaded lake front. A nine-arched loggia forms a porch on the Palazzo di Città, where the tourist office is located.

Omegna's main industry is the manufacture of quality kitchen utensils and cookware, and several companies are based here. **Forum Omegna** is a striking modern showcase for these products, with a museum, a café and a shop selling products of Alessi, Lagostina and others (*Parco Maulini 1. Tel: (0323) 866 141; www.forumomegna.org. Open: Mon–Sat 9am–12.30pm & 2.30–6pm, Sun 3–6.30pm. Free admission*). Alessi, whose innovative cooking, household and tableware is created by some of the foremost contemporary international

Omegna sits at the head of the lake

designers, has a factory showroom where you can purchase current merchandise at discounted prices (*Via privata Alessi, Crusinallo di Omegna. Tel: (0323) 868 611. www.forumomegna.org. Open: Mon–Sat 9.30am–6pm; Dec also Sun 9.30am–6pm*).

Orta San Giulio

Clustered tightly on the shore, from above Orta appears as a solid block of grey stone and red tile. No cars are allowed in the narrow streets, so visitors descend into this medieval town on foot via one of the winding lanes, under overhanging balconies. Via Olina is the main street, running parallel to the lake shore until it reaches the café-encircled expanse of Piazza Motta. Here a new dimension is added to the scene – the deep blue of Lake Orta's waters and the picture-perfect island just offshore. At the water's edge are boats waiting to ferry passengers across.

The frescoed, 16th-century Palazzo della Comunità stands above a loggia at one end, and behind the café tables are smart boutiques and artisans' studios that extend into the side streets. This is a town to wander around, taking your time. Above the town, and reached either by car or by a steep path from Piazza Motta, is **Sacro Monte**, one of several 'sacred mountains' in this region. Inside a nature reserve of beech, pine and lime-tree forests, 20 chapels with terracotta scenes from the life of St Francis line a path through the woods. San Nicolao church and the

View across Orta San Giulio

chapels, built from 1591 to 1770, contain frescoes and 376 statues.

A small tourist office in the 'new' town hall, near the lake shore, has a leaflet describing walking routes around the lake. (In the courtyard there is often a display of sculpture by local artists.) The regional tourist information is at the first car park, above the town.
Ufficio Informazione Turistiche, Via Panoramica. Tel: (0322) 905 163. Open: Mon–Fri 9am–1pm & 2–6pm.

Pettenasco

A short distance north of Orta San Giulio, Pettenasco lies between the road and the shore. The tall, Romanesque tower, visible from the main road from either direction, was once part of the church but was left on its own when the new church was built in the 1700s. The **Museo dell'Arte della Tornitura del Legno** displays various tools and products from the town's woodworking past (*Via Vittorio Veneto. Tel: (0323) 896 22. Open: June–Sept Tue–Sun 9am–noon & 2–6.30pm. Free admission*).

Lago di Lugano

The steep, wooded slopes of Lugano's shore leave room for fewer towns than on Como and Maggiore. Relatively small, at 35km (22 miles) long and 3km (1¾ miles) at its widest, the lake winds in and out of Switzerland, where it is known as Lago Ceresio, with either end in Italy. Most of its tourism is in the central Swiss section. Remember that calls to Swiss locations from abroad are preceded by country code 41.

Lugano

Like an amphitheatre, Lugano rises from the lake front in a bowl shape, parts of the old town so steep that streets become staircases. Its location protects it from harsh Alpine weather, but connects it by rail with the Swiss cities of the north and Milan to the south. An express bus links to Malpensa airport (*www.busexpress.com*).
Turismo di Lugano, Riva Albertolli. Tel: (091) 911 3232; fax: (091) 922 7653; www.lugano-tourism.ch. Open: Apr–Oct Mon–Fri 9am–6.30pm, Sat 9am–noon, Sun 10am–2pm; Nov–Mar Mon–Fri 9am–noon & 2–5pm. A kiosk at the railway station is open Mar–Nov Tue–Sun 2–6.30pm.

Centro Storico

The old streets and arched passageways that radiate from Piazza della Riforma are lined with shops whose smartly dressed customers laden with designer boutique bags mingle with housewives choosing the perfect porcini from quaint little establishments that spill out into the streets. A market fills Piazza della Riforma every Tuesday and Friday morning, and at almost any time you can watch men pondering their next move on the giant chessboard in the adjoining Piazza Manzoni.

Lungolago

Curving languidly around the shore is the tree-shaded Lungolago, a promenade with benches overlooking the water and the mountains.
It connects the two landing piers for excursion boats – Paradiso at the south

end, and the main dock opposite Piazza della Riforma. About halfway between the two, **Giardino Belvedere** provides a green interlude, with rose gardens and flower beds interspersed with sculpture.

Monte Bre

The forested mountain framing the left-hand side of Lugano's Lungolago view is the 933m (3,061ft) high Monte Bre. You can easily ascend to see lake views, an art trail and a village of traditional houses. To reach the funicular, take the No 12 bus from the waterfront to the Cassarate/Monte Bre stop. *Operates: daily 9.15–11.45am & 1.45–4.15pm, 15 June–Sept 9.15am–4.45pm, every 12 minutes.*

Monte San Salvatore

Within walking distance of the Paradiso boat landing and railway station, one of Europe's oldest funiculars ascends the 912m (2,992ft) high Monte San Salvatore. Views open in every direction, sweeping both arms of the lake, Lake Maggiore and a panorama of the Swiss–Italian Alps. Picnic at the top or visit the **Museo San Salvatore**, with minerals, fossils and ecclesiastical art (*Open: Wed–Sun 10am–noon & 1–3pm. Free admission*). A footpath leads to the settlement of Ciona, atop a neighbouring mountain.
Funicular operates: Mar–Nov, every 30 minutes until 11pm.

Santa Maria degli Angioli

The region's finest example of Renaissance art is Bernardino Luini's monumental *Crucifixion*. The fresco, painted in 1525, shows the Crucifixion with scenes from the life of Christ. Luini used his wife as a model, and his own face for that of a Roman soldier. Artists could not sign works in churches, and so such hidden 'signatures' were used.
Piazza Bernardino Luini. For more information, contact Turismo di Lugano (see opposite).

Lake Lugano from Monte San Salvatore

Boat tour: Lake Lugano

A trio of interesting towns lies along the lake close to Lugano, each easy to visit by boat. Unfortunately, they are divided among two routes, one connecting Gandria and another Morcote and Campione d'Italia.

It is possible – with an early start – to combine both trips in the same day and still have time to enjoy some of the shore sights. The trick is to begin by going south to Morcote, skipping Campione and changing boats at the Paradiso landing, where both lines stop, instead of at the main Lugano port. However, it is better to plan one circuit each day or to choose only one. Returns are also possible by local bus. *Navigazione del Lago di Lugano. Tel: (091) 923 1779; www.lakelugano.ch*

An alternative option is to book a private lake tour by vintage mahogany boat, replete with tales of smuggling. The Castelnuovo brothers (*Tel: (091) 967 2013*) know the subject well since their father was a smuggler.

Campione d'Italia

This little enclave of Italy, surrounded by Switzerland on all sides, has an understandably split personality. Vehicles have Swiss licence plates and phones use the Swiss code, yet the official currency is the euro and laws are Italian. The famed *maestri campionese* originated here – a team of architects, artists and sculptors whose church-building skills spread the Lombard style throughout Italy and Europe, rivals of the *maestri comacini* (*see p77*).

Overlooking the shore at the south end of town, **Santa Maria dei Ghirli** is a small chapel with an important 17th-century fresco cycle by Bianchi and elaborate embellishments. The early 8th-century church of San Zeno, now the **Galleria Civica** used for exhibitions, has its original frescoes. But most tourists don't come to see the churches; they come to gamble at the casino and enjoy the lively nightlife in the town's many cafés and restaurants. *Azienda Turistica, Via Volta 16. Tel: (091) 649 5051.*

Gandria

Steps and narrow passages lead between the close-set houses on the narrow

shelf where the town clings. Cantine di Gandria, reached from the lake, is known for its cosy *grotti* – the traditional little restaurants. **Museo delle Dogane Svizzere** (Swiss Customs Museum) is in the former lake customs post at the Swiss–Italian border, and shows boats seized in the act of smuggling.
Tel: (091) 910 4811; www.musee-suisse.ch. Open: daily Palm Sun–Oct 1.30–5.30pm. Free admission.

Morcote

An arcade covers the street along the shore, and antique shops, booksellers and restaurants hide beneath it, making the picturesque little town a pleasant place to stroll. Above, the hillside church of **Santa Maria del Sasso** is well worth the climb for views down into town which, from that perspective,

give a geometric design of roof tiles against aqua-blue water. The church contains some of the region's best 15th-century frescoes, in particular the medallions in the cross vaults and under the arches.

Parco Scherrer is a trip around the world inside a hillside garden. The garden designs, plants, statues, fountains and even buildings reflect times and places from Renaissance Ticino to the Far East. Scherrer collected plants and ideas wherever he travelled, and the result is surprisingly harmonious, seamlessly blending a Thai teahouse, a Greek temple, a little Indian palace and an Egyptian temple each in its own native flora.
Tel: (091) 996 2125. Open: mid-Mar–Oct 10am–5pm; June–Aug until 6pm. Admission charge.

Santa Maria del Sasso overlooks Morcote and Lake Lugano

Train tour: Centovalli

One of Europe's most scenic train rides connects Lake Maggiore's northern shore in Switzerland's Ticino region, with Domodossola, at the foot of the Simplon Pass. The Centovalli (One Hundred Valleys) railway follows the Melezza River and its tributaries, each of which has carved a valley of its own. The 52km (32-mile) railway line, completed in 1928, crosses 83 bridges and passes through 31 tunnels. Vintage railway carriages feature polished wooden interiors and windows that open for photography.

Allow 2 hours for the train ride, and a full day with hikes or excursions.

Two alternatives allow travellers to tailor the trip to their own tastes. An out-and-back trip on the Centovalli line provides time for activities – hiking or exploring small mountain villages. A loop itinerary combining both boat and train gives more variety, but less time to get off the train and explore.

From any point on Lake Maggiore it is possible to take a boat to Locarno, where the train trip begins. From Domodossola, travellers can board the Trenitalia for Stresa, catching a boat back to their starting point. Combined excursion tickets make this easy, and Rail Europe passes are valid on the Centovalli.

First-class passengers can pre-book a substantial lunch of local salamis and cheeses with bread, fruit and wine, or a trolley offers sandwiches. Those planning to explore mountain towns

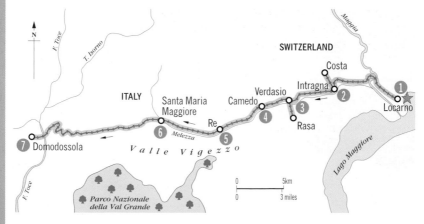

can plan to visit on a market day and buy provisions for a picnic there.

1 Locarno
The trip begins at the railway station, a short walk from the steamer landing. The train emerges from a tunnel onto a terrace overlooking vines.

2 Intragna
The Ticino's tallest church spire marks the entrance to the Centovalli here. From the impressive iron bridge, look back to see an old Roman bridge below. A *funivia* carries passengers to the mountain village of Costa, a 20-minute ride away (*Tel: (091) 756 0400. Operates: Mar–mid-Nov daily 9am–12.40pm & 2.30–6.10pm, every 20 minutes*). Intragna has a small museum of mountain crafts and folklore.

3 Verdasio
Another cable car (*Tel: (091) 756 0400. Operates: daily Mar–Oct 9am–12.40pm & 2.40–6pm, every 20 minutes*) travels across a valley to a high plateau and the village of Rasa, which is accessed only by footpath or cable car. A spectacular trail leads downwards to Costa (*about 2½ hours*), from which a *funivia* returns to Intragna. This requires taking the local train from Locarno, or disembarking at Verdasio, where the Centovalli excursion trains stop, to ride two stops on the next local train, which always leaves 20 minutes later.

4 Camedo
This is the last Swiss stop; Italian border patrols will board to check passports.

5 Re
The domed pilgrimage church is filled with votive offerings to the image of the Madonna, which locals reported seeing bleed after someone threw a rock at her forehead. Saturday is market day.

6 Santa Maria Maggiore
The highest point on the trip, Santa Maria is popular with artists, whose galleries line the streets. The town hall has frescoes and decorative stucco work, and the Chimney Sweeps Museum tells of a traditional local occupation. Monday is market day.

7 Domodossola
The Centovalli trip ends at the railway station, where passengers can connect to the Trenitalia for Stresa or return via the same route with different, eastbound views.

View of Lake Palagnedra from the train

Train tour: Centovalli

Lago di Como

Wealthy Romans decamped from steamy lowlands to the cool of Como's shores, building the first of the lake's long succession of villas. By the 1800s, the lake had become the favourite watering hole of the rich and famous, especially for the British, who continue to favour Como, perhaps the most beautiful of all Italy's lakes.

Long (46km/28¹/₂ miles) and narrow (650m/711yds to 4.2km/2¹/₂ miles), and shaped like an inverted 'Y', Como cuts a deep gash into the mountains that rise steeply on either side. Snow-clad Alpine peaks reflect in the sapphire waters, and the mountains provide a barrier protecting the lakeside from both the harsh Alpine climate and the frequently murky skies of the Venetian plain. Even in winter, Lake Como is temperate, its shores clothed in green and its afternoons often warm enough for tables to be set outdoors in front of terrace cafés.

Pastel-painted villages climb the steep shores, often looking as though they had been arranged there by an artist, who finished the picture by painting green all around them. An astonishing array of villas enjoy these views, and, although few are open, many of their gardens, designed to frame these vistas, can be strolled around. Flowers bloom everywhere, especially in the Tremezzina Riviera.

Explore the lakeside villages on foot to find narrow passages hung with flowering vines. Many buildings rise right from the water, often with arcaded watergates and tiny marinas of their own.

The Romans founded Como as a post on the trade route across the Alps, making it an important crossroads between the Mediterranean, Adriatic and northern Europe. Its former status is best shown by the work of its outstanding school of artists and architects, the *maestri comacini*, whose intricate stone carving is found in churches scattered throughout northern Italy, and worth looking for in even the most modest village churches here.

Roads hug both shores (at frightening altitudes on the section from Como to Bellagio), but the frequent ferry service by both hydrofoils and slower steamers is a good alternative for visiting most of the lakeside towns. Distances are short, and a day's excursion can combine several towns, with time to look around each and to visit attractions. From a base near the centre of the lake, it is very easy to reach all its corners. Many attractions are within walking distance of the ferry landing. Economical day passes allow multiple stops.

Navigazione Lago di Como, Piazza Cavour, Como. Tel: +39 (031) 579 211; www.navigazionelaghi.it

Regular trains and buses connect Malpensa and Linate airports to Milan's Stazione Centrale, from which trains run twice each hour to Como, a ride of about 40 minutes. Shuttle trains from

Excursion boats leave regularly from Como

Lago di Como

Tempio Voltiano in Como

Milan's Stazione Nord arrive at Como's more centrally located Stazione Milano Nord, near the ferry dock, and are timed to meet the ferries. A direct bus from the adjoining bus station connects to Malpensa Airport.

Como

With the lake and mountains beckoning enticingly, it's easy for visitors to hop on to the first boat without stopping to admire the city. That would be a mistake. Not only is Como a pleasant blend of busy, small city and vintage tourist haven; it also has an outstanding, if exuberant, Duomo.

The historic and touristic central section hugs the shore in a warren of streets, all of which seem to lead eventually to the wide and walkable waterside promenade. Café-lined Piazza Cavour is at its centre, near the starting

point for passenger boats. *Como APT (tourist information centre), Piazza Cavour 17. Tel: (031) 274 064, (031) 269 712; www.lakecomo.com. Open: Mon–Sat 9am–1pm & 2–6pm. A smaller kiosk is located on the south side of the Duomo.*

Duomo

Nowhere in Italy can you see a better example of how, in the 14th century, Gothic morphed into Renaissance. In the Duomo, Gothic origins are immediately clear in the richly ornamented marble façade, carved pinnacles reaching skywards and carved figures flanking the entrance. Do note these, for they are not the expected saints, but effigies of the Roman Plinys, both natives. By the 1500s, perhaps everyone had forgotten Pliny the Younger's correspondence with the

Emperor Trajan suggesting reasons for executing Christians. Inside, Gothic elements include the beautiful rose window and deeply carved altarpieces. The St Ambrose altarpiece, in the first chapel on the right, shows the transition from medieval (it's carved in stone) to Renaissance (the polychrome painting). In the next chapel is Luini's *Adoration of the Magi*, one of three Luinis in the cathedral.

Piazza del Duomo. Tel: (031) 265 244. Open: daily 8am–noon & 3–7pm. Free admission.

Museo Civico

From Neolithic artefacts uncovered nearby to memorabilia from the world wars, the Museo Archeologico and the Museo Storico fill two beautiful former *palazzi* with an illuminating picture of the Como region from its earliest history. Roman relics remind visitors that the city's walls were built by order of Julius Caesar. More recent times are covered in exhibits about the work of Garibaldi in unifying Italy.

Via Vittorio Emanuele. Tel: (39) 031 271 343. Open: Tue–Sat 9.30am–12.30pm & 2–5pm, Sun 10am–1pm. Admission charge.

Sant'Abbondio

Although most of the intricate medieval stone carving of the *maestri comacini* (*see p77*) that once decorated this Romanesque church has been taken to the Museo Civico for preservation, the church is well worth

LEONARDO TO JAMES BOND

Como's glamorous scenery has not escaped the attention of artists seeking the right setting. Leonardo da Vinci, who stayed on Lake Como in the late 1400s, used its landscapes as backgrounds for some of his best-known paintings, including *Madonna and St Anne*. More recently, the loggia of Villa Balbianello became the wedding venue for Queen Amidala in *Star Wars*, and the villa was also a hospital for James Bond in *Casino Royale*. Villa Erba in Cernobbio was home to master criminal The Night Fox in *Ocean's Twelve*.

the trip to this deserted part of town. Be sure to see the 13th-century Gothic fresco cycles that transform the apse with vivid colours.

Via Regina (no phone). Open: daily 8am–6pm. Free admission. Bus No 4 or 7 as far as the main train station.

Notable on Como's lake-front **Promenade** (well worth strolling) is the white **Tempio Voltiano**, memorial to native son Alessandro Volta, whose name gives us the word 'volt' (he invented the battery). Near it, almost hidden in a garden, is the sobering and eloquent **Holocaust Memorial**, with quotes from victims in several languages. Further on to the west, the shore is dominated by **Villa Olmo**, whose extensive gardens are a public park. At the opposite end, a funicular ascends to mountain-top **Brunate** (*see p82*).

Funicolare Brunate, Piazza de Gasperi. Tel: (031) 303 608. Open: daily 6am–10.30pm. Admission charge.

An old Lake Como gondola at Villa Melzi d'Eril

Bellagio

Possibly the most perfect setting on Lake Como is reserved for Bellagio, whose streets and gardens rise on the triangular promontory at the centre of the lake's distinctive 'Y' shape. Not exactly undiscovered, Bellagio is well aware of how picturesque it is, but its appeal remains undiminished. Perched on its terraces and lining its narrow streets, candy-coloured buildings house boutiques and cafés, with facing streets that sometimes become staircases. More cafés offer lake views along the waterfront. This is a good place to while away a day or so, with plenty of sightseeing to keep you from feeling lazy.

Bellagio's position at the centre of Lake Como makes it an ideal (if pricey) base for exploring, with boat connections to all three arms of the lake and car ferries shuttling to either shore.
Ufficio Informazioni Turistiche, Piazza Mazzini. Tel: (031) 950 204; www.bellagiolakecomo.com. Open: daily 9am–noon & 3–6pm. Closed: Nov–Mar Tue & Sun.

Basilica di San Giacomo

Above the busy shopping streets, in the historic part of town, the 12th-century Basilica di San Giacomo has a fine triptych by Foppa and a Baroque polychrome sculpture of Christ. Its bell tower was originally one of the town's defensive towers, and was later extended in height to become a campanile for the church.
Piazza del Duomo. Open: 8am–noon & 3–7pm.

Villa Melzi d'Eril

Although this neoclassical villa's interior frescoes are not on public view, its English-style gardens are lovely to walk through. Azaleas and rhododendrons are stunning in the spring, and stately cypresses and exotic plants frame lake views and hide a Japanese garden. A neo-Moorish pavilion sits on the shoreline, and a small chapel and pavilion with changing art exhibitions are open to visitors.

Lungolario Marconi (south on S-583). Tel: (0339) 457 3838. Open: daily Apr–Oct 9am–6pm. Admission charge.

Villa Serbelloni

A lane behind the Basilica di San Giacomo leads to the villa's gardens,

Many of Bellagio's streets are stairways

WALKING AROUND COMO

Dedicated (or even casual) walkers will find paths everywhere that lead to fascinating sights missed by other travellers. An excellent pack of cards, 'By Foot in the Province of Como', with each card detailing a complete walk (in English), is available from provincial tourist offices. With these you can find huge boulders dropped by glaciers, castle ruins, waterfalls, Roman roads and Iron Age rock engravings.

set in a park that crowns the promontory. Italianate 19th-century-style landscaping uses exotic trees as a stage set for views across northern Lake Como, which is backed by the snow-capped Alps. Roses are barely contained between prim box hedges. *Piazza del Duomo. Tel: (031) 950 204. Garden tours: mid-Apr–Oct Tue–Sun 11am & 4pm by reservation; book at the tourist information office in Bellagio. Admission charge.*

The little fishing village of **Pescallo**, the oldest settlement on this peninsula, is a pleasant 20-minute walk from Bellagio, with waterside cafés and *trattorie* (restaurants). For a more strenuous hour's hike with a rewarding view of all three branches of the lake, climb to the belvedere at **Mulini del Perlo**. Walk a little further to **Chevrio-Makalle** for another panorama. By car, follow the narrow mountain roads to San Primo, where you can ride the cable car up **Monte San Primo**, or climb to the summit from the end of the road. Winter visitors can ski there.

Southern Lake Como

The lake's western arm begins at the city of Como and includes some of its least-visited towns. Discouraging vehicles from travelling between Como and Bellagio is the vertiginous road, in places barely wide enough for two cars.

Brunate

Rising at gradients as steep as 55 per cent, a century-old funicular climbs more than 1,000m (3,281ft) from Como's lake front to give fantastic views of the lake and mountains. Café terraces in the precipitous village offer views to the south, but to see the Alps and the lake-shore towns to the north, you must climb the stone-paved path to the tower at the top. Once there, to save climbing the 143 tower steps, enjoy the same view in comfort from a café table at La Regonda.

Funicolare Brunate, Piazza de Gasperi. Tel: (031) 303 608.

Villa d'Este's elaborate gardens

www.funicolarecomo.it. Open: daily 6am–10.30pm. Admission charge.

Cernobbio

The S-340 road follows Como's western shore to Cernobbio, whose lake front is dominated by villas. The most elegant of these is **Villa d'Este**, designed in the late 16th century by Pellegrino Tibaldi. Formerly home of English Queen Caroline, it is now a sumptuous hotel, surrounded by elaborate Italianate gardens. **Parco di Villa Erba**'s gardens are open to the public on weekends.

*Via Regina 2. Tel: (031) 34 91. www.villadeste.it.
Open: Sat 2–6pm & Sun 10am–6pm. Free admission.*

North of town is the road to **Monte Bisbino**, a 1,355m (4,446ft) high mountain with a road to its summit and spectacular panoramas of both Italy and Switzerland. The Swiss boundary is near the mountain top. Just beyond the turn-off is **Moltrasio**, known for its gardens and the 11th-century church of **Sant'Agata**.

Ufficio Turistico, Via Regina 33, Cernobbio. Tel: (031) 510 198.

Nesso

Unless you catch a quick glimpse of the arched stone bridge as you pass through Nesso on the S-583, you might not be tempted to stop. But those who have first seen Nesso from the lake steamer's infrequent stops know that far below the road is one of the loveliest vignettes on the lake. Follow the steeply

Nesso sits astride a deep gorge with a Roman bridge at its foot

descending cobbled streets and stone stairs along the south side of the deep rocky ravine, which slices the town in half, to emerge at lake level. Here, centuries-old stone buildings rise out of the water, and the Nose River is spanned by a Roman bridge. Deep inside the ravine there is a spectacular waterfall.

Unfortunately, the boats do not stop here but at the town docks further north, from which you must climb to road level before descending again into the cleft. Nevertheless, they do pass tantalisingly close for good, if fleeting, views of this enchanting spot.

Just south is **Careno**, a tiny moss-covered stone settlement clinging to the steep lake shore. The Romanesque church of San Martino is reached by a steep path from the road above.

Torno

This medieval village at a bend in the lake is known for Villa Pliniana, built in the 16th century at the spot where Pliny the Younger had earlier built a villa. A cascade there still turns on and off at regular six-hour intervals, just as Pliny described it. Stop at the church of San Tecla to see its outstanding Romanesque carved portal.

Villa Carlotta is known for its gardens

The Tremezzina Riviera

The mildest shores of this calm-weather lake are along the central western shore, in an area known as the Tremezzina Riviera. Lush foliage encases the hillsides and wraps itself around the villas. Palms, camellias and exotic trees thrive here, many of them far north of their usual range. Like Bellagio, this makes a good central base from which to explore by car or boat, with frequent steamer and hydrofoil services and a car ferry connecting to Bellagio in the centre and Varenna on the eastern shore.

Ufficio Turismo, Via Regina 3, Tremezzo. Tel: (0344) 404 93; www.tremezzina.com. Open: May–Sept Mon–Wed & Fri–Sat 9am–noon & 3.30–6.30pm.

Villa Balbianello

Spread luxuriantly across the end of a peninsula are the immaculately groomed grounds of a Baroque villa, built for Cardinal Durini in the 1700s. Lawns slope gently down towards the lake, bounded by a sculpted stone fence, from whose top rail life-sized statues gaze across the lake. Each massive tree and blossoming shrub is placed to frame the lake and mountain views. Lake steamers pass close enough for an enticing preview of the villa from the water. Like other gardens in the region, these are at their most flamboyant from late April through to mid-June, when azaleas and rhododendrons are in full bloom. But with or without the flowers, Villa Balbianello and its gardens are considered to be the lake's most romantic spot.

Visits to the gardens begin in nearby Lenno, from where boats depart during the garden's opening hours. It is also possible to visit the gardens on foot (it is less than a 1km/^{2}/3-mile walk) from Lenno on Tuesdays, Saturdays, Sundays and holidays.

Tel: (0344) 561 10; www. fondoambiente.it. Open to boat arrivals: mid-Mar–Nov Tue & Thur–Sun 10am–6pm. Open to visits on foot: same hours Tue, Sat & Sun. Admission charge.

Also in **Lenno** is the 11th-century church dedicated to Santo Stefano, which has an interesting octagonal Romanesque baptistery behind it. In 1945, Mussolini and his mistress were killed in Mezzegra, a short distance inland, after their capture at Dongo on the northern shore of Lake Como.

Villa Carlotta

Taking full advantage of the Tremezzina's mild temperatures, Villa Carlotta, a 17th-century palace bought as a wedding present for the Prussian Princess Carlotta, has one of northern Italy's most celebrated gardens. Originally planted in the 1850s, its camellias, rhododendrons, azaleas and exotic trees line broad paths, and open to a succession of lake views backed by mountains. Although the 5.6 hectares (14 acres) of gardens are the best reason for visiting, the villa itself is open as a museum of sculpture (with several pieces by Canova) and paintings by the Lombard masters. Its interior decorations are 18th century.

Via del Regina. Tel: (0344) 404 05; www.villacarlotta.it. Open: daily Apr–Sept 9am–6pm; Mar & Oct 9–11.30am & 2–4.30pm. Admission charge.

The villa is on the way to Cadenabbia, just north of Tremezzo, an easy, pleasant walk along the shore promenade – an occasionally interrupted alley of plane trees known as **Via del Paradiso**. Up the hill in Griante is the cone-topped church of **San Martino**, set on a scenic terrace overlooking the lake.

Tremezzo's lakeside is lined with beautiful villas

Isola Comacina

A great deal more is unknown about the troubled and eventful history of Isola Comacina than is known. Throughout its story weaves a who's who of famous names – Queen Theodolinda, Frederick Barbarossa, King Albert of Belgium, Vittorio Emanuele II's daughter and saints Abbondio, Agrippa and Domenica.

The island seems to have been a hotbed of religious fervour, as the presence of three saints would attest. By the time the barbarian hordes swooped in from the east, the tiny island already had five churches on it, at least one thought to have been a temple built by the Romans and subsequently consecrated by Christians.

Certainly Comacina was inhabited in Roman times, and probably long before that, since its steep shore was easily defended. On the arrival of the first barbarians, wealthy Christians escaping Como took refuge here, naming it Christopolis and waiting out the attacks of Attila the Hun and the Goths who succeeded him.

When the Lombards conquered northern Italy in the 6th century, the Byzantine governor managed to escape to Isola Comacina, bringing with him his considerable treasure and reinforcing its fortifications. This aroused the interest of the husband of Lombard Queen Theodolinda, who besieged and conquered the island, sparing its inhabitants but seizing the treasure.

In turn, the Lombard King Berenger II took refuge there in AD 962, as did the Holy Roman Emperor Frederick Barbarossa in the 12th century. The island became known as a place of refuge, even peace, and Sant'Abbondio and at least two others found sanctuary there. It was Abbondio who brought the cult of Santa Eufemia to the island, and initiated the building of the largest church, a basilica dedicated to her.

The islanders' unwise siding with Milan in the rivalry between that city and Como was their undoing. Although Milan eventually won the day, Como was the closer neighbour and razed the island in 1169. As for the inhabitants, they either were killed or took flight. The ruins that resulted from the attack are what we see today on the now deserted island.

Touring the island

A single trail loops around the island. Following it uphill leads along the crest of the highest point, and to the foundations of **Santa Maria col Portico**, with olive trees growing among its stones. Beyond here the trail descends to reveal the best view of the remaining group of churches. Of the medieval **Basilica di Santa Eufemia**, low walls and stone floors remain to show its layout in a little glen below the later Baroque **Oratorio di San Giovanni**, which is still standing.

Easy to miss behind the oratory is the **Palaeo-Christian baptistery**, with mosaics from the 5th to the 9th centuries and frescoes from the time of Charlemagne, in geometric patterns. The island is an atmospheric place to take a picnic lunch and, perhaps, to wander with ghosts from the Middle Ages.

Boats shuttle back and forth from Sala Comacina, where there is ample parking uphill from the S-340. *Tel: (0338) 459 9492. Operating: daily Mar–Oct 10am–4.30pm. Regular lake steamers also stop at the island. Navigazione Lago di Como. Tel: (031) 579 211; www.navigazionelaghi.it*

The ruins of Basilica di Santa Eufemia below the Isola Comacina's only remaining church

Orrido di Bellano

Northern Lake Como

The landscape becomes less precipitous along the northern shore of the lake. Some of the most interesting attractions – a 13th-century abbey and a deep chasm carved in solid rock – are in this region.

Abbazia di Piona

The 13th-century abbey surrounds a fine Romanesque cloister, showing the beginnings of the Gothic style. Delicate columns end in capitals with detailed carving in a wide variety of motifs. Frescoes date from the 14th and 15th centuries, and more cover the sanctuary of the adjoining 11th-century church of San Nicola. Cistercian monks at the active monastery grow medicinal herbs and produce the cosmetic creams, honey and liqueurs sold in the shop.
Open: daily 8.30am–12.30pm & 1.30–7pm. Free admission.

Bellano

The most outstanding natural wonder on Lake Como is the long and convoluted **Orrido di Bellano**, a deep gorge sculpted into potholes and caves by the River Pioverna. Seen from the safety of walkways high above river level, the gorge has a waterfall in its centre. *Tel: (338) 325 7117. Open: Apr–June daily 10am–1pm & 2.30–7pm; July–Sept daily 10am–1pm, 2.30–7pm & 8.45–10pm; Oct–Mar Sat, Sun & holidays 10am–12.30pm & 2.30–5pm.*

Beside the steps leading to the Orrido stands the early Gothic church of **Santi Nazaro e Celso**. The mid-1300s façade of striped stone features a rose window. The frescoes in the nave are remarkable examples of *trompe l'œil*, fooling the eye into seeing flat walls as statuary, balustrades and relief carving.

Gravedona

One of Lombardy's major Romanesque sites, the 12th-century church of **Santa Maria del Tiglio** has a free-standing octagonal bell tower, with early frescoes of St John the Baptist and a section of floor revealing mosaics from the 5th-century previous structure. The inside of the tower is completely open and almost severe, the large fragments of fresco giving an inspiring impression of how it must have looked when the entire interior was covered with them. *Via Roma. Open: Mon–Fri 3–5pm, Sat & Sun 10am–6pm. Free admission.*

Menaggio

Smart cafés surround the lakeside Piazza Garibaldi in the historic centre of this attractive resort. Less 'mature' than the Tremezzina, Menaggio has a better selection of restaurants. The road to Lake Lugano climbs (stop for lake views at **Croce**), then levels out to Portelezza. Just north, in the village of Nobiallo, the **Santuario della Madonna della Pace** sits tranquilly among olive and cypress trees, perhaps the loveliest setting of any church on the lake.

Varenna

Clustered under cliffs, Varenna appears from the lake to be a geometric pattern of pink, red, gold, cream and ochre stucco with a green surround. A lakeside promenade bordered with colourful flowers connects the ferry landing to the town centre. The convent of **Villa Monastero**, abandoned in the 16th century, provides terraces of formal gardens filled with Mediterranean and exotic plants.

Tel: (0341) 295 450; www.villamonastero.it. Open: daily 9am–noon & 2–7pm (5pm off-season).

Above the city, the 11th-century **Castello di Vezio** has a falconer and falcons demonstrating this medieval art.

Via Esino Lario. Tel: (0348) 824 2504; www.castellodivezio.it. Open: Apr–Oct daily 10am–6pm, later during June–Sept; Nov–Mar weekends only. Admission charge.

Cloister of Abbazia di Piona

Agritourism

Farmhouse bed and breakfasts, country restaurants that serve meals made from home-grown ingredients, beekeepers with roadside kiosks, horse-riding ranches, farms with camping sites – all these small rural enterprises are promoted in Italy under the banner of *agriturismo* (agritourism). The initiative is a happy one for those travellers who delight in meeting local people and eating wholesome local dishes.

Added to this is the knowledge that the money spent helps to maintain a way of life that is often endangered in the modern world. Frequently, this extra income from tourists provides the margin to keep a family farm alive. Some enterprises may seem no more than a crowded backyard garden, but it may surprise you to learn how self-sufficient a family can be on a small plot of land.

Each region has its own directory of these establishments, and those with guest rooms are listed in the back pages of local accommodation guides. The range of activities you can enjoy at farms is wide. Some invite you to take part by milking the cow or helping in the grape harvest, although you are never expected to work unless you wish to. All will enjoy sharing the workings of their operation – a tour of the barns, a walk in the orchard or vineyard, a pony ride for the children, or the opportunity to watch milk become cheese. And you may be sent off with a bag of freshly picked cherries, a jar of honey or a sausage from the smokehouse.

Rooms may be simple and comfortable, either in a section of the farmhouse or in purpose-built accommodation on the property. Alternatively, you may find yourself in a vintage family villa, especially in the rich farmlands of the Mantova region. These are often a distance from towns with restaurants, and so many provide a hearty farmhouse dinner in the evening, or have a full restaurant

Agritourism sign in Angera

Agriturismo Fioravante

of their own. All include breakfast, and you can depend on the fruit jams being home-made.

Often situated at the end of country lanes, these farms may be tricky to find, but if you book in advance they will send maps, or you can ask at the nearest village if you miss a signpost.

For illustrated directories of properties, including restaurants, accommodation and farm shops, contact the following agencies:
APT del Mantova (tourist information centre), Piazza Mantegna 6. Tel: (0376) 328 253; fax: (0376) 363 292. Associazione Agriturismo Trentino, Via J Aconcio 13, 38100 Trento. Tel: (0461) 235 323; fax: (0461) 235 333; www.trentinoagritur.it Regione Lombardia Direzione Generale Attività Produttive – Servizio Promozione, Via Sassetti 32, 20124 Milano. Fax: (02) 676 562 94; www.lombardia-agriturismo.com

Agriturist Veneto, Via Monteverdi 15, 30170 Venezia Mestre. Tel: (04) 292 249; fax: (04) 292 456.

Agriturismo Fioravante
A small Valpolicella winery, close to Verona. *Via Don C Biasi 7, 37020 San Floriano, Verona. Tel: (045) 770 1317; fax: (045) 770 1317.*

Camping Clarke
Camping site on a small farm with horses, other animals and fresh eggs, south of Bellagio. *Località Visgnola. Tel: (031) 951 325.*

Locanda Mose
High above Lake Como, with guest rooms, camping site and a restaurant specialising in products of the farm, which include ricotta and freshly picked berries. *Località Pian di Nesso. Tel: (031) 917 909. Open: all year. Closed: Wed.*

Entrance to a farm guesthouse near Lake Garda

Bergamo

Bergamo has a decidedly split personality. The new city spreads on the flat plain while, above it all, the regal old city – the Città Alta – is encased in high walls. The lower city is only new by comparison: it was built after the medieval and Renaissance streets and piazze of the upper city.

At the centre of Bergamo's Città Alta is a beautiful ensemble of Renaissance buildings around a sloping *piazza*, and through the loggia at the top is another *piazza* surrounded by churches and related buildings. Cutting through the centre of the old city, Via Gombito is a narrow medieval lane lined by shops, churches and tiny squares. Most of the city's prime sites are in this old hilltop town.

Uffici di Informazione Turistica: Città Alta, Via Gombito 13. Tel: (035) 242 226; www.turismo.bergamo.it, www.italiantouristboard.co.uk; Città Bassa (lower city), Piazzale Marconi. Tel: (035) 210 204. Open: daily 9am–12.30pm & 2–5.30pm.

Funicular

This is the easiest and fastest way to get from Viale Vittorio Emanuele II, in the Città Bassa at the foot of the hill, to Piazza Mercato delle Scarpe in the Città Alta, the old town at the top of the hill. It runs on rails and is pulled by dual

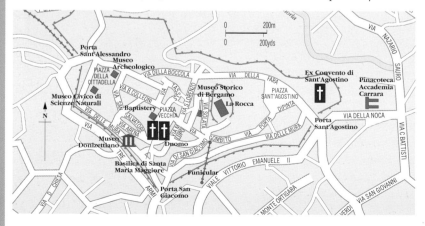

cables, rising at an ever-increasing gradient through the massive walls. *Viale Vittorio Emanuele II. Tel: (035) 236 026; www.atb.bergamo.it. Open: Mon–Sat 10.15am–8pm, Sun & holidays 7.40am–12.10pm; runs every 15 mins (buses run at other times). Tickets are valid for the funicular and any bus fare in the same zone for an hour.*

Pinacoteca Accademia Carrara

The generous Giacomo Carrara gave not only his entire collection of paintings to the city in 1796, but the neoclassical building as well. With the addition of other collections, the Accademia now houses more than 1,600 paintings and other collections of sculpture, drawings, prints, medals, porcelains and bronzes. Look for everything from Angelico and Botticelli to Pisanello, Rubens, Raphael and Van Dyck. The gallery covers three floors, with the primary collections housed on the second and third floors. There are seven closed rooms on the first floor containing about 600 paintings that can be seen by request. The **Galleria d'Arte Moderna e Contemporanea** (GAMEC, *Via San Tomaso 53; tel: (035) 270 272; www.gamec.it; admission charge*) is dedicated to the visual arts of the 20th century. It concentrates on Italian artists, but also has works of non-Italians. The collections include De Chirico, Kandinsky, Morandi, Bale and Casorati. *Piazza Giacomo Carrara 82A. Tel: (035) 399 677;*

www.accademiacarrara.bergamo.it. Open: June–Sept Tue–Fri 10am–9pm, Sat 10am–11pm.

La Rocca

Bergamo's castle is a hard, uphill walk but well worth it for the view over the old town alone. Site of the Roman Capitolium, the castle was begun in 1331 and finished by the Visconti in 1336. Blown up in 1511 by lightning and again by the French, it was later occupied by the Venetians and the Austrians, serving as a prison and place of execution for Garibaldi's followers until he liberated it in 1858. World War I armaments are found in a courtyard. A former military school in the grounds used to be a museum of the Risorgimento but has been closed; there are plans to reopen, but no date is set. *Piazzale Brigata Legnano. Tel: (035) 221 040; www.museostoricobg.org. Grounds open: Tue–Sun 9.30am–1pm & 2–5.30pm (June–Sept Sun 9am–7pm).*

Bergamo's Città Alta sits above the newer town

Piazzetta Duomo

The small square behind Piazza Vecchia – the Piazzetta Duomo – and the adjoining Piazza Giuliani contain a trove of Bergamo's treasures. This is the probable site of the Roman forum and the medieval 'People's Assembly', and it is now flanked by the cathedral and a clutch of other ecclesiastical buildings.

Aula della Curia

Upon entering this hall, you will be transported to the 13th century. The arch and all of the frescoes date from that period, and the whole ensemble is intact. The building served as the entry hall to the diocesan curia.
Enter from either Via San Salvatore or Piazza Vecchia.

Baptistery

Originally inside the Basilica of Santa Maria Maggiore, the 14th-century baptistery was taken down after 1659 and put away in storage. Two hundred years later it was reassembled, but dissatisfaction with its location led to its second disassembly and reconstruction here in 1898. Slender columns line its octagonal top, along with eight 14th-century statues of the Virtues. The font with bas-relief of the life of Christ is also octagonal, and is by Giovanni da Campione.
Open for baptisms only.

Colleoni Chapel

Next to the north portico of the basilica stands the late Gothic Colleoni Chapel, the mausoleum of Bartolomeo Colleoni who was a 15th-century *condottiere*, the protector of Venetian interests in the area. Designed by Giovanni Amadeo, much of the exterior sculptural work is also by him. Inside, the tomb reflects the outsized ego of the warlord. The frescoes are by Giovanni Battista Tiepolo, and were completed in 1733. The tomb of Bartolomeo Colleoni's 15-year-old daughter, Medea, was moved here in the 19th century.
Tel: (035) 233 327. Open: Tue–Sun 9.30am–12.30pm & 2–4.30pm.

Duomo

The neoclassical façade of the cathedral of Sant'Alessandro dates from 1886, but

The portico of Santa Maria Maggiore

the interior is Baroque. To the left of the door is Moroni's *Madonna and Child*, and on the main altar the second painting to the left is Tiepolo's *Martyrdom of St John, Bishop*. Tel: (035) 210 223. Open: daily 7.30–noon.

Santa Maria Maggiore

Begun in 1137, the basilica is considered one of the finest Romanesque works. The main entrance in red, white and black marble is the work of Giovanni Campione. A loggia holds a mounted St Alexander flanked by two saints; the smaller loggia above was added in 1396. Along the walls to the left is a minor portal topped by a crucifix also by Campione, as is the south portico, a tall arched canopy supported on columns that rest on the backs of standing lions and crouched telamons. Above is a frieze of Christ and the twelve Apostles, with saints on the side. The iron strips affixed to the walls were medieval units of measure. Inside, the outstanding wood inlay work on the presbytery stalls is by Lorenzo Lotto, one of the masters of inlay.
Tel: (035) 223 327. Open: Mon–Sat 9am–12.30pm & 2.30–6pm, Sun 9am–1pm & 3–6pm.

Tempietto di Santa Croce

Opposite the southern entrance of Santa Maria Maggiore, this is a tiny gem of Romanesque architecture. It was built in the 10th century and restored in 1561.

The Gothic Colleoni Chapel

Via San Salvatore. Tel: (035) 237 279. Open: by appointment, exterior always visible.

Musei Civici

There are three civic museums in Bergamo. Two are situated in the Piazza della Cittadella near the western end of Viale della Mura, approached through the 1355 **Torre della Campanella** (Tower of the Little Bell). Inside the courtyard is the **Museo Archeologico** with a collection of artefacts dating from prehistoric through to Lombard times. Off the same courtyard is the **Museo Civico di Scienze Naturali**. It

Contarini Fountain in Piazza Vecchia

has extensive collections of specimens, more than 10,000 lepidoptera, a herbarium with 4,000 species, fossils (including the flying dinosaur reptile *Eudimorphodon ranzii*) and a reconstructed mastodon. The **Museo Storico di Bergamo** presents the history of Bergamo through a collection of artefacts.

Museo Archeologico, Piazza Cittadella 12. Tel: (035) 242 389; www.apt.bergamo.it. Open: Tue–Sun 9am–12.30pm & 2.30–5.30pm. Free admission.
Museo Civico Scienze Naturali, Piazza Citadella 10. Tel: (035) 233 154. Open: Tue–Fri 9am–12.30pm & 2.30–5.30pm, Sat & Sun 9am–7pm. Free admission.
Museo Storico di Bergamo, Convento di San Francesco, Piazza Mercato del Fieno
6/A. Tel: (035) 247 116; www.perfiloepersegni.it. Open: Tue–Sun 9.30am–1pm & 2–5.30pm. Free admission.

Museo Donizettiano

The great opera composer Gaetano Donizetti lived and worked in Bergamo, and two rooms of an 18th-century palace commemorate his life. His birthplace in a street nearby, which shows the extreme poverty from which he ascended, can be visited by appointment.

Via Arena 9. Tel: (035) 428 4769. Open: Tue–Fri 9am–1pm, Sat & Sun 9.30am–1pm & 2–5pm. Free admission. Birthplace: Via Borgo Canale 9. Tours by appointment only.

Piazza Vecchia

This is about as close to a perfect Renaissance square as will be found anywhere. In the 15th century, a warren of buildings was removed and the civic building, the 12th-century **Palazzo Ragione**, was rebuilt to face the new square. Its covered staircase was added in 1453, and the loggia in 1520. The main room has significant 13th-century frescoes, but is open only during exhibitions. The tall clock tower in the corner (**Torre Civica** or **Il Campanone**) dates from the 12th century and was a Ghibelline stronghold (*see p127*). The clock still rings curfew at 10pm. Along the western side is **Palazzo Podestà**, former home of the Venetian Governor. At the north end is the white, marble-faced **Civica Biblioteca A. Mai**, housing 1,274 incunabula among its collections. In the centre is the beautiful **Contarini Fountain** presented to the city in 1780, with fantastic lions, serpents and sphinxes.

At the intersection of Via Gombito and Via Colleoni.

Torre. Open: Mon–Fri 9.30am– 7pm, Sat & holidays 9.30am–9.30pm.

Admission charge.

Viale delle Mura and the gates

Use Viale Vittorio Emanuele II for the best road access to the Città Alta. At the end there is one of the original gates to the walled city, **Porta Sant'Agostino**. Inside the gate, Viale delle Mura begins, running inside the town wall on the eastern, southern and western sides. Immediately at the right of the gate is the Convent of St Augustine, which is used for exhibitions, and a large promenade created in the 1880s. Straight ahead, Viale delle Mura turns into Via della Fara and leads to **Porta San Lorenzo**, the gate through which Garibaldi entered the city.

On the southern side, about midway along Viale delle Mura, is another gate – **Porta San Giacomo**. Viale delle Mura meets up with Via Tre Armi, which runs at the foot of the hill, at its western end at **Porta Sant'Alessandro**.

Gateway to the castle, Bergamo

The Venetian empire: looking for lions

The symbol of St Mark is the lion, and both the saint and his symbol are inextricably tied to Venice and the Venetian empire, which stretched across northern Italy to include Brescia and Bergamo. Venetian lions can be found all across the Mediterranean, too. Although the boundaries of the present-day Veneto have receded somewhat and the region begins at the western shore of Lake Garda, traces of the lion remain in the lands once controlled by La Serenissima – the Venetian Republic.

The lion often stood atop a column, as he does in Verona's Piazza delle Erbe. However, these types of lion have disappeared outside the Veneto region, and you are more likely to find the lion carved in bas-relief on a prominent wall overlooking a square, or on the arch over a gate.

The Venetian lion is easy to distinguish from just any old lions that might embellish a fountain, or guard an entrance. First, he is winged and he always holds (or originally held, if

If the book in the lion's paw is open, Venice was at peace when he was carved

the carving has been damaged) a book in one paw. If the book is open, Venice was at peace when he was carved there. When the book is closed, Venice was at war.

Many of these lions have gone, some deliberately defaced or removed when the Venetians left town. Others have fallen victim to war, neglect or development. Yet a non-violent form of lion hunting will turn them up, sometimes in unexpected places such as carved on a pulpit. Scan old *piazze* and the courtyards of medieval and Renaissance town halls. In Brescia's Broletto (*see p106*) you can see where a lion has been almost entirely defaced.

Bergamo retains a classic lion of St Mark at the main entrance to the old city, where the street passed through Porta Sant'Agostino (*see p97*). Above the gate, a large lion is carved, open book in paw. At night, when the gate is bathed in floodlights, you can see it from the lower town. In Rovereto (*see pp130–31*), St Mark's lion on the old city gate reminded those who entered that they were in a city belonging to La Serenissima.

Also in Bergamo, a relief panel of the lion of St Mark faces the Piazza Vecchia, a prime example of how these were placed to remind the populace of who was in control.

Venetian-style windows face the Duomo in Brescia

Another clue that a city was once Venetian – or at least had a strong Venetian influence – is a triple set of arched windows, separated by delicate columns. Look for these in Brescia's Broletto and the building surrounding the clock tower in Piazza Loggia. In Mantova you will see them on one wing of the Ducal Palace. The style is very common in Verona, where you will see these windows on many buildings, but especially in Piazza dei Signori (*see p137*). You can find this style in the towns around Lake Garda as well.

Excursion: San Pellegrino and the Val Brembana

Few places evoke the Belle Époque, in all its fading grandeur, quite like the spa town of San Pellegrino. The springs of this town are the source of the world-famous water, whose familiar label shows the turreted spa that made the town a mecca for the rich and famous in the early 20th century.

Although the grandest of the hotels have closed, enough remains of the architecture, the splendour and the spa's easy ambience to reward a trip there. And for anyone who loves Art Nouveau architecture, this town rates a gold star on the map of Europe.

The valley in which San Pellegrino lies, the Val Brembana, is pretty itself, although the river scenery is marred with hydropower plants below San Pellegrino. Some distance up the valley beyond, the road snakes up the Passo San Marco, the only road to scale that wall of mountains. Centuries of traders have followed this tortuous route, but the mountains are now the realm of hikers, climbers and skiers.

The whole region is filled with small farms, many of which welcome visitors to buy their fresh baked goods, wines, cheese and fruit.

San Pellegrino

After an unpromising entrance to the town, past the enormous bottling plant for the famous mineral water, the S-470 becomes San Pellegrino's main street. The town climbs the hill on the western bank of the Bremba, connected by a wide bridge to the Art Nouveau railway station and the massive Grand Hotel.

The hotel, stucco crumbling and with its great wrought-iron canopy rusting away, stands brooding over the river. If an antiques show or other exposition is happening there, seize the chance to see the interior, where an enormous spider chandelier hangs in the entrance hall, and the stucco work and ceilings are in surprisingly good condition.

Opposite, San Pellegrino has coped better with the vicissitudes of fashion, its arcaded buildings in good repair, and the town is lively with cafés and shops. Behind and above is the casino, with its towers and stone frills. Reached through well-kept gardens, a wide terrace fronts the casino, theatre and arcaded Terme San Pellegrino, the spa.

The façade of the casino is decorated with every imaginable embellishment, and the inside of this astonishing wall of stonework is no less amazing – an entrance hall in textbook Art Nouveau. The walls are stencilled in the familiar floral scroll panels, and every detail is in period. But this pales beside the grand salon ahead, where a split staircase rises into an almost hysterical outburst of decoration, featuring every Art Nouveau motif and medium.

The spa is still operating, both in the elegant old building adjoining the casino, with its wall fountains, and in the stylish modern spa across the street below. You can drink from the springs, swim in the elegant pool, take the cure for gout or indulge in therapeutic baths, wraps and massages.

Via Taramelli 2. Tel: (0345) 224 55; www.sanpellegrino.it. Open: Tue–Sun 8am–noon & 3.30–6.30pm. Pool open: Tue–Sun 11am–7pm. Admission charge.

The home of the famous mineral water

Lago d'Iseo

West of Lake Garda and easily reached from both Bergamo and Brescia, Lake Iseo has been a summer haven for the cities' noble families, who built villas on its shore. Before that it was a centre of commerce with the north, and home to fishermen.

Although often maligned for the industry at its perimeter (mixed manufacturing), which is in fact confined to cities at either end of the lake, Iseo still has most of its shore intact. In the north, vertical limestone cliffs drop into the water, and along the southern shore is a nature reserve known for its profusion of water lilies, which bloom spectacularly in the spring.

The claim to fame for this small lake is the mountain that rises out of its centre, forming a cone-shaped island. The castle-topped mountain – Monte Isola – is the largest freshwater island in Europe. Also outstanding are the hundreds of prehistoric pictographs in the Val Camonica, north of the lake, which are protected by a National Park.

A 60km (37-mile) road encircles the lake, whose towns can also be reached by ferries and tour boats with dining facilities, operated by **Gestione Navigazione Lago d'Iseo**.

Via Nazionale 16, Costa Volpino. Tel: (0359) 714 83; fax: (0359) 729 70.

You can reach Lake Iseo from Bergamo or Rovato (on the main Milan–Venice train line) via the **Treno Blu**, a tourist railway that runs to Sarnico, where it links with the boats for a tour of the lake and Monte Isola. A day excursion includes train, boat to Monte Isola, and lunch.
*Tel: (030) 740 2851; www.ferrovieturistiche.it. Buy tickets on board or at **Clio Viaggi** (www.clioviaggi.com).*

Rock art at Capo di Ponte

Capo di Ponte

The human occupation of the **Val Camonica**, north of the lake, dates at least from the Bronze Age, and is demonstrated by the hundreds of images carved into the rocks by prehistoric peoples. **Parco Nazionale delle Incisioni Rupestri** protects a huge mountainside area of these at **Capo di Ponte**. Incised in the exposed rocks, which are well connected by pathways, are deer, labyrinths, ladders, hunters and alphabets. A map with descriptive information is available in English. The little museum describes what is known of the lives of prehistoric peoples through dioramas and artefacts. Parking is along the S-42, with a trail up to the park. In the off-peak seasons, there is parking closer to the entrance.

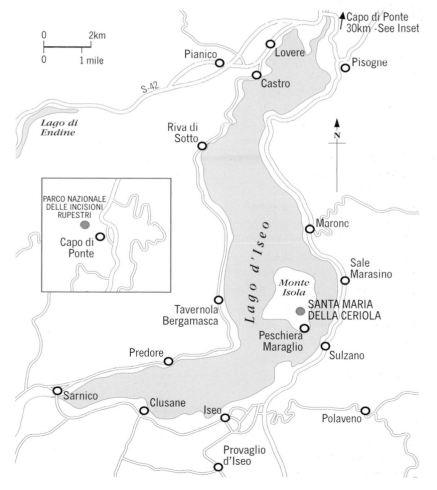

The tiny village of Vello clings to the side of Lake Iseo

S-42. Tel: (0364) 421 40. Open: Mar–mid-Oct Tue–Sun 8.30am–7.30pm. Admission charge.

The Romanesque **Monasterio di San Salvatore**, built in the 11th and 12th centuries, has beautiful stone carvings, as does Capo di Ponte's parish church of **San Siro**, also 11th-century Romanesque. Monasterio di San Salvatore, Capo di Ponte. Open: daily 9am–noon & 3–6pm. Admission charge.

Clusane

On the southern shore, west of Iseo, Clusane is a small and attractive fishing port known for its restaurants specialising in lake fish. Looming over the shore is the boxy Castello del Carmagnola.

Iseo

Since the pre-Christian era – at least as far back as 400 BC, when Celtic peoples inhabited the area – Iseo has been an important trading centre for goods produced by the entire region. From prehistoric times the Camonica Valley, north of the lake, was a busy highway and, until a shoreline road and a railway were built in the 19th century, the lake carried traffic from the valley to Iseo. Today it is the headquarters for tourism, with its compact town centring on Piazza Garibaldi. The beautiful **Lungolago Marconi** is a promenade around the shore, with cafés and views of the lake, and it is a favourite spot for local shore fishermen.

Azienda Promozione Turistica, Lungolago Marconi 2. Tel: (030) 980 209; www.comune.iseo.bs.it. Open: daily 10am–12.30pm & 3.30–6.30pm.

Castello Oldofredi, now housing the town's cultural centre and library, dates from the 11th century but was rebuilt in the 14th (Via Mirolte. Open: Mon–Fri 9am–noon & 2–5pm). The 12th-century church of **Sant'Andrea** has an original Lombard Romanesque bell tower, and the tomb of Giacomo Oldofredi is built into its outside wall.

Monte Isola

In the middle of Lake Iseo, Monte Isola is the largest lake island in Europe, and has retained its air of an insular fishing community possibly because no private vehicles can go there. A small bus connects the towns, which lie among vineyards and groves of chestnut and olive trees. The 14th-century **Rocca Martinengo** (north of Sensole) and another **Castello Oldofredi** (outside Peschiera Maraglio) once protected the island. The church of **Santa Maria della Ceriola** is a pilgrimage site because of a venerated wooden statue of Mary. On the top of the mountain, it can be reached by bus from Cure in the summer.

Fishing and fish curing are still active industries on the island. You can visit the curing houses and perhaps see people making or mending fishing nets. The island fishing cooperative offers boat tours from Sulzano that include visits to a shop that makes fishing nets, a wooden boat builder, and a close-up look at the two small, privately owned islands near Monte Isola.
Barcaioli Piccola Società Cooperativa, Monte Isola. Tel: (0347) 819 9172/ (0335) 844 0916. Open: by appointment.

The island has good hiking trails and narrow roads where cyclists do not have to contend with traffic. A ferry service to Peschiera Maraglio and Sensole operates from Sulzano, on Lake Iseo's eastern shore. Ferries to Carzano leave from Sale Marasino. Both are frequent.

Ufficio Turistico Peschiera, Peschiera Maraglio. Tel: (0309) 825 088.

Pisogne

At the northern end of the lake, Pisogne is a small town with attractive arcaded buildings. On the road towards Fraine, the former monastery of **Santa Maria della Neve** has an outstanding cycle of frescoes by one of the region's best-known artists, Girolamo Romani (Romanino). Locals call this 'the poor man's Sistine Chapel'.
Tel: (0364) 870 32. Open: Tue–Fri 3–5pm, Sat & Sun 9.45–11.30am. If closed, ask at the Romanino Bar next door.

San Pietro in Lamosa

Off the old road south of Iseo, overlooking the lake and nature reserve west of Iseo, is the 12th-century monastery of San Pietro in Lamosa. Along with its setting and views, it is worth visiting for its fine 15th-century frescoes.
Provaglio d'Iseo. Tel: (030) 983 477.

Lago d'Iseo

The harbour at Clusane

Brescia

An often overlooked city, Brescia was one of the earliest Roman settlements in the north. Its sights, from the ancient forum to its Novecento Piazza Vittoria, show more than two millennia of architecture and art.

Broletto

The centre of public life while Brescia was a city state, the Broletto remained in this role when the Venetians took over in the 15th century, and the building is still in government service. Three sides of its internal courtyard are medieval and the other has a 17th-century colonnade.

Piazza Papa Paolo VI, across from the Duomo. Courtyard open: normal workdays.

Capitolium and the Piazza del Foro

Brixia, as the Romans called it, was by the 1st century AD a major city filled with important buildings. In its forum, Vespasian erected the Capitolium in AD 73, but it was destroyed by fire in

Tourist office. Piazza della Loggia.
Tel: (030) 240 0357; www.bresciatourism.it.
Open: Apr–Sept Mon–Sat 9.30am–6.30pm;
Oct–Mar Mon–Fri 9.30am–5pm,
Sat 9.30am–12.30pm.

the 5th century. Rediscovered in 1823, it was partially reconstructed in 1939. Original components of white marble in the columns and pediment are easy to distinguish from the brick used in reconstructed parts. Portions of the arcaded forum have been excavated to reveal former Roman shopfronts, and, while you cannot wander around in these, everything is clearly visible.

Via dei Musei 55. Tel: (030) 297 7834.
Open: Tue–Sun 11am–6pm.
Free admission.

Castello

Atop Cidneo Hill, where the Celts once built their town, the castle offers spectacular views over the city. Thick brick walls tower over a dry moat and the tall, round Prisoner's Tower commands the entrance. Inside, the former Venetian grain store is now the **Museo del Risorgimento**, which is dedicated to the period of Italian unification. The Visconti Keep houses

the **Museo delle Armi Luigi Marzoli**.
Its ten rooms, some decorated with
14th-century frescoes, hold an
incredible collection of Italian and
European arms from the 14th to the
18th centuries.
*Cidneo Hill (by car from Piazza Cesare
Battisti or Piazza Arnaldo). Castle open:
Oct–May Tue–Sun 9.30am–5pm;
June–Sept Tue–Sun 10.30am–6pm.
Museo del Risorgimento, Via Castello 9.
Tel: (030) 441 76;
www.bresciaholiday.com. Open:
Oct–May Tue–Sun 9.30am–5pm;
June–Sept Tue–Sun 10am–6pm.
Admission charge.
Museo delle Armi Luigi Marzoli,
Via Castello 9. Tel: (030) 293 292;
www.bresciamusei.com. Open: Oct–May
Tue–Sun 9.30am–5pm; June–Sept
Tue–Sun 10am–6pm. Admission charge.*

Decumanus Maximus

Brixia's forum was located on the
Decumanus Maximus, the most
important city road. At the foot of the
stairs leading to the Capitolium, a
section of the original road has been
exposed where it runs past the arcaded
fronts of Roman shops.
Via dei Musei, Piazza Foro.

Duomo Nuovo

This is the 'New Cathedral', but new is
relative. The church was begun in the
17th century, the huge cupola being
completed in the early 19th century.
The last altar on the right-hand wall is
the tomb of Sant'Apollonio and has an
excellent *Last Supper* painted on wood
below. Under the dome, the four
Evangelists appear with their symbols.
*Piazza Paolo VI. Tel: (030) 427 14.
Open: Mon–Sat 7.30am–noon &
4–7.30pm, Sun 8am–1pm & 4–7.30pm.*

Duomo Vecchio

Next door is the Romanesque 'Old
Cathedral' from the 12th century, with
9th- and 11th-century crypt and
medieval frescoes. This is one of the
few round early Christian churches
remaining intact. In its rotunda, eight
trapezoidal pilasters manage to support

The restored Capitolium

the cupola. A number of 16th- and 17th-century paintings by Romanino, Moretto and Francesco Maffei can be found in the chapels.

Piazza Paolo VI. Tel: (030) 427 14. Open: Apr–Oct Tue–Sun 9am–noon & 3–7pm; Nov–Mar Sat & Sun 9am–noon & 3–5pm.

Piazza del Foro

This *piazza* covers the site of the forum – the focus of city life during the period of Roman rule from roughly the 1st century BC until the 5th century AD. Here, the Roman road Decumanus Maximus (now Via Musei) and the city's next most important street, Cardus Maximus (Via Laura Cereto), met. At the top of the *piazza* are the Capitolium and the church of San Zeno in Foro (18th century).

Piazza Loggia

Only a short walk from the Piazza Vittoria, Piazza Loggia provides a great contrast. While Piazza Vittoria is an entire ensemble of Novecento, or Fascist, architecture, entering Piazza Loggia is like stepping into the Renaissance, an open expanse with arcaded buildings at either end. It takes its name from the 15th-century Palazzo Loggia, in whose design both Sansovino and Palladio had a hand. The unusual

Brescia's Romanesque Duomo Vecchio

roof was added in 1914, allegedly designed after a period print. Across the *piazza* is the Torre dell'Orologio (Clock Tower) in a Venetian-style arcaded building from the 15th century. Two human figures strike the 1518 bell. The tourist information office is in the old Monti Pietà (Pawnbrokers), an attractive 16th-century building.

Pinacoteca Civica Tosio Martinengo

The gallery in the 15th-century Martinengo *palazzo* displays a collection of 13th- to 18th-century Italian paintings, including many by major Brescian artists. There are works by Raphael, Veneziano, Solario, Lotto, Romanino and Moretto. Many of the works were originally in churches and private collections.

Piazza Moretto 1.
Tel: (030) 377 4999;
www.bresciamusei.com. Open: June–Sept Tue–Sun 10.30am–6pm; Oct–May Tue–Sun 9.30am–5pm.
Admission charge.

Santa Giulia Museo della Città

Located in the former convent of Santa Giulia, this is the home of Roman Brixia. The treasure trove of Roman antiquities (over 11,000 pieces) includes a Winged Victory (actually a 3rd-century BC Greek piece), mosaic floors, fragments of columns and other decorative detail that was uncovered during extensive excavations. The interiors of two 1st-century Roman houses include frescoed walls and mosaic floors. The wonderful museum brings together a tremendous wealth of other artefacts from the city's history, brilliantly interpreted and displayed.

Via Musei 81b. Tel: (030) 297 7834;
www.bresciamusei.com
Open: June–Sept Tue–Sun 10am–6pm; Oct–May Tue–Sun 9.30am–5.30pm.
Admission charge.

Teatro Romano

Excavations of Roman Brescia continue, and at the east end of the Capitolium is the Flavian-period (AD 69–96) Roman theatre, which originally sat 15,000 people. In its upper section was a brick ambulatory, and below a hall of pillars still joins it to the Capitolium. Much of the theatre's seating remains, as well as parts of the underpinnings of the stage area.

Not open to the public but visible from Vicolo Fontanone.

The Renaissance clock in the Torre dell'Orologio

Walk: Brescia

Brescia's two millennia of sights are neatly packaged into two clusters, connected by a street that follows the ancient Roman main road. A parking garage is hidden under Piazza Vittoria, making it a good place to begin, even though it means walking backwards through history.

Allow 2 hours' walking time, plus stops.

Start in Piazza Vittoria.

1 Piazza Vittoria

A complete square of Novecento (Fascist) buildings, the *piazza* includes an often overlooked detail of the era, a balcony for addressing crowds. This one is an unusual red, marble carved 'pulpit'. *Walk to the right of the striped postal building, following Via Post through the arch to reach Piazza Loggia.*

2 Piazza Loggia

Imbedded into the southern wall are stones from earlier Roman buildings,

which were put there in 1480. There is a distinctly Venetian look to the Torre dell'Orologio, atop which two *macc de le ure* (crazy timekeepers) ring out hours (*see p109*).
Walk through the arch under the clock, bearing right. Turn left and then right onto Via dei Musei. Turn right towards Piazza Papa Paolo VI.

3 Broletto

On the left of Piazza Papa Paolo VI (named after Brescian Pope Paul VI) are

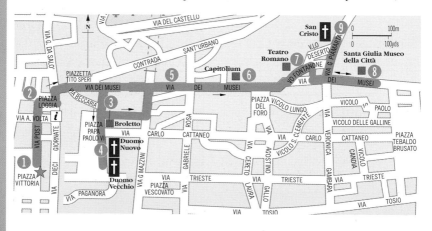

the 13th-century tower and government buildings of the city state (*see p106*).

4 Duomo Nuovo and Duomo Vecchio

Beyond the Broletto are these two cathedrals, side by side. This is slightly unusual, since new cathedrals were more often built on top of the earlier ones (*see pp107–8*).
Leave the piazza from the end you entered, going right through the arch and arcaded courtyard of the Broletto. Turn left onto Via G Mazzini, then right onto Via dei Musei.

5 Via dei Musei

Following the Roman high street, Decumanus Maximus (parts of which lie buried beneath), the street is lined with *palazzi*. Stop at the courtyard of Palazzo Martinengo Cesaresco, on the right. Churches on this street have brown historical signs in English.
Continue towards Piazza del Foro.

6 Capitolium

Standing above the forum, the temple has been reconstructed to show four of its six columns and much of its

Clock tower on Piazza Loggia

pediment. A segment of original street and parts of the forum are excavated (*see p106*). You can admire this ensemble from the Caffè Caligola.
Turn left at the end of the excavated area on Vicolo Fontanone.

7 Teatro Romano

Built into the hillside (parts of which buried it in a landslide), much of the amphitheatre is visible (*see p109*).
Follow Vicolo Fontanone, turning right again to rejoin Via dei Musei, heading left.

8 Santa Giulia Museo della Città

Inside former convent grounds, the new museum of art and history has excavated two rooms of a major Roman house, over which the convent was built in AD 753 by Desiderius, King of the Lombards (*see p109*).
Retrace your steps to Via G Piamarta, turning right.

9 San Cristo

Two other churches are incorporated into the complex, and the façade of one is visible from Via Piamarta. This 15th-century monastery has a pretty cloister and interesting marble carvings on its portal. More carvings are found on the outside of the apse behind the church, and inside it is richly frescoed.
Return along Via dei Musei, crossing Via G Mazzini to Piazzetta Tito Speri. Beyond, a left turn enters Piazza Loggia, which leads back to the starting point.

Lago di Garda

While the Italians share Lakes Maggiore and Lugano geographically with the Swiss and Lake Como historically with the British and Americans, they share Lake Garda with the British, Germans and Austrians. In waterside restaurants and cafés you're as likely to hear a foreign language spoken as Italian at neighbouring tables. Despite this influx of tourism from the north through the Brenner Pass, Garda retains its Italian character, especially on its western shore.

The largest of Italy's lakes, Garda covers more than 350sq km (135sq miles), and is 83km (52 miles) long. Narrow at the northern end, where it is hemmed in by mountains, the lake widens to the south, with a shoreline of gently rolling hills. Its beauty has inspired writers since Goethe's time (German tourists are not a new phenomenon) and perhaps D H Lawrence, who lived in Gargnano and described the lake most lyrically in *Twilight in Italy.*

This lake, like the others to the west, enjoys a mild year-round climate, so the vegetation that surrounds it – palms, olives and lemons – grows further north than is usual. The road that encircles the lake is the most scenic in the mountainous north, but much of it runs through tunnels along the northwestern shore. If circling the lake, the scenery is best when driven in an anticlockwise direction, travelling north along the

Breathtaking scenery around Lake Garda

east side and south on the west. Traffic is heaviest around the southern part of the lake.

Every town of any size is connected to the others by boats that circle the lake, and shorter shuttles are provided between nearby towns. Southern towns have more options; in the north there may well be a long wait for the next boat circling the lake.

Navigazione Lago di Garda.
Tel: (030) 467 6101 or freephone 800 551 801; www.navigazionelaghi.it.
Check website for timetables.

Limone sul Garda has a tiny enclosed harbour

Riviera dei Limoni (The Lemon Riviera)

No one claims that Garda's northwestern shore is undiscovered, and cafés and boutiques are plentiful along the narrow lanes of candy-coloured houses. Yet that does not diminish the charm of the easy lakeside promenades of its towns. Connected by the SS-45, which spends more time in tunnels than revealing lake views, these towns are well worth exploring.

Gardone Riviera

If Gardone seems to lack cohesion, blame its geography. The narrow space between the water and the road, coupled with the enormous garden that is the town's steeply sloping centrepiece, makes it hard to fit in much else. The result is two towns, one a promenade of well-dressed, Belle Époque hotels and villas along the shore, and the other the hill-top **Gardone di Sopra**, whose picturesque square faces **Il Vittoriale** (*see pp116–17*). Between lies **Giardino Botanico Hruska**, 10,000sq m (12,000sq yds) of botanical gardens. Cascading in terraces of exotic trees, plants from every continent thrive around pools, fountains and sculptures in the mild lake climate.
Via Roma. Giardino open: daily Mar–Oct during daylight hours.

A public park surrounds **Villa Alba**, built as the summer estate of the German Kaiser Wilhelm II. **Torre San Marco**, the stone tower of its dock, is a landmark on the shore below. Gardone's promenade is a pleasant place to while away the early evening.
Comunità del Garda, Via Mirabella, Gardone Riviera. Tel: (0365) 290 411; www.lagodigarda.it

Limone sul Garda

Protected by the knife-sharp stone ridges behind it, Limone long ago turned its sheltered slope into terraced lemon groves. Tourism has largely replaced lemons, but some still grow along the shore and above the town's winding lanes of pastel-coloured stucco buildings. A large car park at the information kiosk on the SS-45 handles the overflow when the more convenient one at the end of Lungolago Marconi, the long lakefront promenade, is full. Shopping, cafés and strolling past the little Porto Vecchio are what Limone is all about. A car ferry connects to Malcesine from the south end of the Lungolago Marconi.

Ufficio Informazioni Turistiche, Lungolago. Tel: (0365) 954 265.

Salò

Sitting at the end of a long bay, Salò is the largest town on the eastern shore. Its claim to historic fame is as the site of Mussolini's puppet republic in the final years of World War II. The **Duomo** has a splendid gilded wooden altarpiece and choir, as well as a wealth of Renaissance paintings, including several by Romanino. Unfortunately, it is so poorly lit that the paintings are all but impossible to see. The Renaissance portal is all the more noticeable because it stands in a still unfinished façade.

Vicolo Campanili. Tel: (0365) 521 700. Open: daily 9am–noon & 3.30–6.30pm. Ufficio Informazioni Turistiche,

Piazza Sant'Antonio. Tel: (0365) 214 23; www.lagodigarda.it. Open: daily in summer.

Toscolano-Maderno

The highlight of these twinned villages is the 12th-century Romanesque church of **Sant'Andrea**, whose interior frescoes and fine stone carving have unfortunately not been accessible since the closing of the church after structural damage in the November 2004 earthquake. But the wonderful stone carving around the front door is still visible, and well worth stopping to see. Fantastical creatures, intricate knotwork and a myriad of other carved stone detail not only surround the door but decorate other parts of the façade. Notice the inscribed Roman stones used in the construction – an early example of recycling.

Piazza San Marco.
Ufficio Informazioni Turistiche, Via Sacerdoti 1. Tel: (030) 374 8741.

Altar of Salò's Duomo

Il Vittoriale

Il Vittoriale is designed in Art Deco style

For the last years of his life, the highly gifted poet and writer Gabriele d'Annunzio devoted his attention to his villa high above Lake Garda – Il Vittoriale. There, with his friend the architect Gian Carlo Maroni, he created an Art Deco never-never land to house his collections and indulge his decorating whims. If in the process he created a monument to himself, he at least ensured that he and his work would be remembered.

Il Vittoriale is not easy to forget. The interior is open only with a guided tour, necessary to navigate the maze of connecting rooms and passageways, and to find the truly significant pieces amid the jumble. The tour tells something of the poet's life and exploits of derring-do, to put the artefacts in perspective.

The music room is draped in black – even the ceiling, where the curtains and a large snakeskin are suspended on gold cord. The few lights are muted by glass shades. The dark was not altogether a product of d'Annunzio's gloomy psyche. He had lost an eye in a World War I flying accident – he was a decorated pilot – and the remaining eye was left photophobic, making dark far more comfortable for him.

A veranda off the bedroom – stuffed with china knick-knacks and heaped with dozens of silk pillows – contains a rare glimpse of personal items: a photo of d'Annunzio's mother and of his earlier love, actress Eleanora Duse. An unexplained Little Red Riding Hood doll sits in a bird bath. Some 900 objects decorate one bathroom, in which the dark-blue Art Deco bathtub matches the sink and bidet.

Perhaps the most curious room contains a hard bed, where d'Annunzio lay to contemplate the meaning of death. Here his body lay for a night of vigil after he died, aged 74, at his desk in the small study. His work, long shunned due to his Fascist associations, is back in fashion. He had written speeches for Mussolini in the early days, but later became more critical, fuelling Il Duce's worst fears and sealing d'Annunzio's virtual house arrest here.

Mussolini feared that this charismatic war hero who had once stirred the patriotic emotions of the Italian people with his words and his audacious feats (he led a squadron over Vienna to drop inflammatory pamphlets) might do so again, and not to Il Duce's benefit. Thus, he showered d'Annunzio with laurels, named him president of the Italian Royal Academy, proclaimed his villa a national monument, and made sure he stayed there.

Il Vittoriale sits in a hillside park, on whose gardens d'Annunzio lavished as much unrestrained largesse as he gave the house. A ship is embedded into the hillside as a memorial to two comrades who died in the private invasion of Fiume (where d'Annunzio and his followers set up their own government). Above, his mausoleum rises, tier upon tier, to a surmounting plinth on which rests his tomb.

Il Vittoriale degli Italiani, *Via Vittoriale, Gardone di Sopra. Tel: (0365) 201 30. Grounds and house open: daily Apr–Sept 8.30am–8pm; Oct–Mar 9am–5pm. Museum open: daily Apr–Sept 9.30am–7pm; Oct–Mar Tue–Sun 9am–1pm & 2–5pm. Admission charge.*

D'Annunzio's tomb surmounts a gigantic mausoleum

The Northeast Shore and Monte Baldo

Two castles, one set majestically on a high point above the lake, Alpine scenery and lovely little harbours full of bright boats give variety to the northeastern shore. This is where Lake Garda suddenly narrows to the mountain-bound terrain common to the other lakes. The resulting wind currents make the shore popular with sailors and windsurfers, while the long ridge of Monte Baldo attracts walkers.

Brenzone

Dotting the lake shore with its colourful little villages, Brenzone's prettiest spot is hidden from the S-249, but the little river that cascades past the road marks its location. Park in the tiny *piazza* south of the cascade and walk beside the river to the charming little port. Here, a bridge arches across the stream that opens into a little harbour surrounded by brightly coloured houses. A round stone tower guards the far side, punctuating one of the lake's most photogenic ensembles.

Malcesine

On a rounded peninsula, backed by Monte Baldo and faced across the lake by some of the most rugged and beautiful shoreline, Malcesine is a match for its setting. Cobbled medieval streets wind upwards, past art studios and small shops, to **Castello Scaligero**, which perches on a cliff high above the lake. In the 1780s, German poet Goethe was arrested as a spy for drawing a picture of it, but photographers and artists are safe there today. Castles don't get better surroundings, and beaches don't get any better views than that of the tiny cove at its foot, reached by steep steps from Via Posterna. Inside the castle, a museum displays some of Goethe's drawings. *Tel: (045) 657 0333. Open: daily mid-Mar–Oct 9.30am–8pm (last admittance 7.30pm); Dec–mid-Jan 10am–5pm; mid-Jan–mid-Mar Sat & Sun only. Admission charge. Closed: Nov.*

There is a covered car park on the hillside above the S-249, and a car ferry crosses the lake from Malcesine to Limone sul Garda. *Ufficio Informazioni Turistiche, Via Castello & Via Capitano. Tel: (045) 740 0044/(045) 740 0837; www.malcesinepiu.it*

Monte Baldo

Views of the lake and to the pre-Alp and Dolomite peaks are a ten-minute ride from Malcesine. A modern 360-degree, windowed *funivia* (cable car) carries passengers up Monte Baldo to 1,650m (5,400ft) for panoramas and access to the walking trails along the ridge. Monte Baldo is known for its abundance of Alpine wild flowers. In winter, the *funivia* becomes a ski lift leading to smaller lifts that reach 11km (7 miles) of upper snowfields. *Funicolari Malcesine–Monte Baldo. Tel: (045) 740 0206. Operates: daily Apr–Oct 8am–6pm, June–mid-Sept until 7pm.*

Torri del Benaco

The 14th-century **Castello Scaligero**, built (like most castles in this region) by Verona's della Scala family, overlooks a little marina. Its Museum of Natural History exhibits flora and fauna of the Garda.

Tel: (045) 740 0837. Open: Dec–Jan daily 9.30am–4pm; Feb–Apr Sat & Sun 11.30am–4.30pm; May–Nov daily 9.30am–6pm. Admission charge.

A ferry carries cars across the midpoint of the lake to Gardone Riviera.

Lago di Garda

Malcesine sits on a peninsula, crowned by a castle

Riviera degli Ulivi (The Olive Riviera)

Olive groves, growing far north of their usual range, give the gentle hills here a soft green colour, and their name – the olive shore. Although this is the most heavily visited part of the lake, the Riviera's former fishing towns are attractive and well kept – which is why so many people come here.
www.rivieradegliulivi.bs.it

Bardolino

Bardolino's shaded benches invite visitors to enjoy the view of the lake front. A cycling and walking path follows the lake shore from Bardolino to Torri del Benaco, and passes the car park just north of the town. Most streets between the S-249 and the promenade are closed to all traffic.
Ufficio Informazioni Turistiche, Piazzale Aldo Moro. Tel: (045) 721 0078; www.lagodigarda.it

Two early churches are close to the main road. The 9th-century Carolingian **San Zeno**, although well signposted, is rarely open, but the 11th-century Romanesque **San Severo** usually is. Easy to spot by its tall, cone-topped tower, San Severo preserves many original frescoes and some excellent early stone carving on the capitals. The crypt below the altar (be careful of the well-worn steps) has intricate knot designs carved in its posts.

The region's olive groves give rise to a major local olive oil industry, explored in the **Museo dell'Olio d'Oliva** on the S-249 just south of the town (and difficult to enter and exit by car). Here you can compare flavours, buy olive products and tour the excellent displays. Early presses and containers illustrate the origins of olive oil, and visitors learn that the tree is not native to Italy but was spread around the Mediterranean by the Romans.
Via Peschiera 54 (S-249), Cisano di Bardolino. Tel: (045) 622 9047; www.museum.it. Open: Mon–Sat 9am–12.30pm & 2.30–7pm, Sun & holidays 9am–12.30pm. Free admission.

Bardolino is best known for its red wine, which has its own interesting,

Marina at Lazise

Romanesque frescoes cover San Zeno's interior

although less ambitious, **Museo del Vino** at the Zeni winery. English signage describes winemaking methods, and artefacts include presses and tools from the 1800s, and Roman and Etruscan amphorae. Summer wine-tasting evenings need to be pre-booked.
Via Costabella 9. Tel: (045) 721 0022; www.museodelvino.it. Open: mid-Mar–Oct daily 9am–1pm & 2–6pm. Free admission, charge for tastings.

Garda

Garda is purely for pleasure, a place to sit in a café or on a lakeside bench and enjoy the view. Or, for the more active, walk or cycle along the shore path to **San Vigilio**, a scenic point with a pebble beach and beautiful views past a 16th-century *palazzo* and tall cypresses.
Ufficio Informazioni Turistiche, Via Don Gnocchi 25. Tel: (045) 627 0384; www.aptgardaveneto.com

Lazise

A tidy marina with bright boats sits alongside an arcaded Venetian customs house and a 12th-century stone church, **San Nicolo**, interesting for its frescoes. The inevitable Scaligeri castle, from the 11th century, is not open to visit.
Ufficio Informazioni Turistiche, Via Fontana 14. Tel: (045) 758 0114; www.lagodigarda.it

Orto Botanica del Monte Baldo

Specimens of Monte Baldo's abundant indigenous Alpine plants, including edelweiss and Alpine lilies, thrive in these botanic gardens, reached by following the signposted road from Garda to Caprino Veronese. At Spiazzi, the sanctuary of **Madonna della Corona** overlooks the Adige Valley to the east.
Ferrara di Monte Baldo. Tel: (045) 624 7065. Open: daily May–mid-Sept 9am–6pm.

Riva and the Garda Trentino

The River Sarca flows into Lake Garda from between two mountain ranges that protect the river's valley from Alpine cold. Since prehistoric times, this mild climate has attracted settlement, and its many castles attest to the valley's importance as a trading route.

Ufficio Informazioni Turistiche,
Largo Medaglie d'Oro, Riva del Garda.
Tel: (0464) 554 444;
www.gardatrentino.it

Arco

Curling around a shaft of vertical cliffs, Arco's old town centre would be a pleasant place to wander even without its castle. On top of the cliffs stands **Castello d'Arco** with a room of 14th-century frescoes that illustrate medieval court games and chivalry. Stairs and a path climb the slightly gentler western slope.

Ufficio Informazioni Turistiche,
Via delle Palme 1. Tel: (0464) 532 255.
Open: daily Apr–Sept 10am–7pm;
Oct–Mar 10am–4pm (fresco room closes one hour earlier).

Also on the western side of town, the **Arboreto di Arco** contains exotic trees that flourish in the valley's unusually mild microclimate.

Via delle Palme. Open: daily Apr–Sept 9am–7pm; Oct–Mar 9am–4pm.

Castello Drena

Hanging above the Salagoni Gorge, the walls and tall single tower of Drena date back to the 1100s. Inside,

Hotel Sole overlooks the boat landing at Riva

a museum shows Bronze Age archaeological finds from the valley. *Tel: (0464) 541 220. Open: Apr–Oct Tue–Sun 10am–6pm; Nov–Mar Sat & Sun 10am–6pm. Admission charge.*

Ceniga

North of Arco, the River Sarca is spanned by a Roman bridge, **Ponte Romana**. Beside it a little picnic area is shaded by olive trees. Bordering the narrow lane, an amazing assortment of fruits grow – kiwi, bananas and figs, along with the expected grapes. **Sentiero delle Marocche**, a mountain hiking trail, begins at the bridge.

Riva del Garda

Monte Brione rises precipitously from Riva's old town, which crowds between the cliff and lake. At its heart, Piazza III Novembre is surrounded by café-filled colonnades and the 13th-century Torre Apponale (Clock Tower) that chimes the hour. The *piazza* opens onto the lake at the passenger boat landing. A shore promenade leads past parks and glorious formal gardens to the nearby town of **Torbole**, the windsurfing capital of the lake.

The castle **Rocca di Riva** sits on a little island formed by its own moat. It houses an excellent museum on the prehistoric settlements here that has unusual Copper Age stelae, and a collection of medieval armour. *Museo di Riva del Garda, Piazza Cesare Battisti 3A. Tel: (0464) 573 869; www.comune.rivadelgarda.it. Open:*

Arco's castle stands above the town centre

Tue–Sun 10am–12.30pm & 1.30–6pm. Admission charge.

A pleasant all-day excursion on the lake is offered on the sailing ship *Siora Veronica*, which sails (*daily, 8.30am*) from the castle moat's inlet. *Tel: (0335) 548 3030; www.letsgosailing.it*

Plunging from a lake through a 100m (328ft) deep vertical hole in the rock, **Cascata del Varone** is possibly Italy's most dramatic waterfall. English signs explain how the water's force carved the corkscrew-shaped tunnel, creating an ecosystem so cool and wet that it has its own flora. *Via Cascata 12 (Tenno). Tel: (0464) 521 42; www.cascata-varone.com. Open: May–Aug 9am–7pm; Apr & Sept 9am–6pm; Mar & Oct 9am–5pm; Nov–Feb 10am–5pm. Admission charge.*

Southern Garda

Some of the busiest lake towns are on its southern shore, but here also is the lake's prize town, Sirmione.

The Valtenesi – the hilly region between the lake and the valley of the Chiese River to the west – is a land of farms, vineyards and olive groves, its scenery often bordered by ridge lines of dark cypress trees. This is just the antidote for the busy roads and beaches of the southern shore.

The best beach along the Valtenesi shore is south of Manerba (follow signs to the *spaggia* (beach)). A long beach with more facilities, but also more people and less atmosphere, is at Lido di Lonato, where there are tent pitches.

Castle towns of the Valtenesi

Castles seem to crown every high point along the lake's shore and into the hills that rise behind it. However, from below the passing traveller cannot see that some of these contain whole villages snugly encased inside the walls. *ProLoco Manerba, Via Risorgimento, Manerba del Garda. Tel: (0365) 551 121; www.gardavaltenesi.com*

Inside the square castle at **Moniga del Garda**, starched rows of brightly painted houses line the outer walls to form a tiny city. A larger fortress, surrounded by olive groves, tops the hill at **Padenghe sul Garda**, reached by Via Castello. From the summit there are views across the lake, and hidden inside is an entire town of stone houses, their backyard vegetable gardens tucked against the warm stones of its wall. The castle is large enough for the town to have three long parallel streets and a fully grown pomegranate tree in one garden. The fortress was begun in the 10th century, but the present walls are from the 14th century.

Amid the rolling vineyards of the Valtenesi hills, to the west of Lake Garda, no town hides inside the walls of the castle at **Soiano del Lago**. Its courtyard is used for concerts in the summer, and a nature park starts at the long alley of cypress trees that leads from its gate.

Desenzano del Garda

Conveniently located at the base of the lake, and the lake's only town with a train station, Desenzano makes an ideal base, especially for those using public transport. The A-4 *autostrada* (motorway) is also close. Shops and restaurants surround the pretty marina, and castle ruins top the town's low hill. An excavated Roman villa, **Villa Romana**, has some excellent mosaics. *Via Crocefisso 22. Tel: (030) 914 3547. Open: Mar–mid-Oct Tue–Sun 8.30am–7pm; mid-Oct–Feb Tue–Sun 8.30am–4.30pm. Admission charge.*

Look into the parish church of **Santa Maria Maddalena** to see the painting *The Last Supper* by Tiepolo. The **Museo Archeologico Rambotti** has Roman artefacts and those from earlier peoples. *Viale Tommaso dal Molin. Tel: (030) 914 4529. Open: Tue–Sat 9.30am–12.30pm & 2.30–5.30pm. Admission charge.*

The fishing harbour at Desenzano del Garda

Tuesday is not a good day to drive into Desenzano, since the weekly market covers the entire waterfront with stalls selling everything from Valtenesi farm cheeses to jewellery. *Ufficio Informazioni Turistiche, Via Porto Vecchio 34. Tel: (030) 914 1510; www.gardalake.it*

Peschiera del Garda

Since the Romans first settled at Lake Garda, everyone has had a hand in fortifying Peschiera, which is where the River Mincio flows from the lake. The last were the Austrians, who in the mid-19th century beefed up the walls the Venetians had built in order to protect Peschiera from Italians set on independence. A century later, the Germans moved in, using the charming old *palazzo* as their command headquarters during World War II.

La Rocca, the 2,300m (2,500yds) of fortifications, surrounds the old port

Gelati in every conceivable flavour tempt visitors to Sirmione

Lago di Garda

with grass-topped walls that form a bridge at the end of the colourful marina. Arriving from the A-4 motorway, bear left through the main gate, **Porta Verona**.

Complesso Monumentale. Open: daily 9am–12.30pm & 2.30–6pm. Admission charge.

There is a car park on the lake front at the port, opposite the APT tourist information office.

Piazzale Betteloni 15. Tel: (045) 755 1673; fax: (045) 755 2901; www.peschieradelgarda.org. Open: Mar–Oct Mon–Sat 8am–1pm & 3–6pm, Sun 8am–1pm. Closed: Nov–Feb Sun, Mon & pm.

Sirmione

The Romans were the first to take their holidays at the tip of the 3km (2-mile) long tongue of land that juts into the centre of the lake. Built in the 1st century AD, **Grotte di Catullo** was an exceptionally large villa in an exceptionally beautiful location. Surrounded by olive trees at the very tip of the peninsula, it includes the ruins of arches, a hall, a swimming pool and a corridor overlooking the lake. The museum houses the archaeological finds.

Tel: (030) 916 157. Open Tue–Sun 9am–dusk. Admission charge.

A dozen centuries later, the della Scala family of Verona defended the entrance to the town with a castle, **Rocca Scaligeri**, still in excellent condition. The moat around the castle makes an island

---

SCALIGERI CASTLES

You may notice in northern Italy, especially in the region once controlled by the powerful della Scala family of Verona, notched crenellations on top of castle walls. This 'fishtail' shape is typical of a medieval political group called the Ghibellines, supporters of the old feudal aristocracy and the Emperor. Opposing them were the Guelphs, the rising middle class who supported the Pope in the constant tug-of-war between Church and temporal power. Whenever you see these notched crenellations, you can be sure the builders were Ghibellines, and around Lake Garda most likely Scaligeri.

---

of the town. Inside the double row of defensive walls there is a museum of Roman and medieval archaeological finds, but the main attraction of the castle's interior is the view at the top. A harbour inside the castle's outer walls provided safe refuge for village fishing boats and the Scaligeri fleet.

Tel: (030) 916 468. Open: Apr–Sept Tue–Sun 9am–7pm; Oct–Mar Tue–Sun 8.30am–4.30pm. Admission charge.

Between the castle and the Roman villa is a town filled with designer shops and *gelati* (ice cream) bars. Among all this hides a trio of churches, the oldest of which is the 8th-century **San Pietro**, with 12th-century frescoes.

Ufficio Informazioni Turistiche, Viale Marconi 2 (by the bus station and main car park). Tel: (030) 916 114 or 916 245; www.comune.sirmione.bs.it. Open: Apr–Oct daily 10am–7pm; Nov–Mar Mon–Fri 9am–12.30pm & 3–6pm, Sat 9am–12.30pm.

Driving tour: Lake Idro route

A scenic circular tour from Salò reaches two lakes that are seldom visited by tourists. The steep mountainsides vary from wooded to almost vertical cliffs falling on either side. A few sections of steep, winding road are not for those with vertigo, but the route is well maintained and the scenery unparalleled. A long tunnel bypasses the steepest portion. The most frustrating thing about this trip will be the scarcity of lay-bys from which to take photographs.

Allow 1–2 days if stopping overnight somewhere.

Begin south of Salo from the S-45b, following brown signposts along the Chiese River to 'Val Sabbio'.

1 Lago d'Idro

The first views of this long, narrow lake are above the town of Idro, at its southern end. An attractive picnic site with a children's playground overlooks the lake beside the road. Ahead, the northern end of the lake disappears into a series of steeply sloping mountainsides. At an altitude of 370m (1,214ft), Idro is the highest Lombardy lake.

2 Anfo

Plenty of tourist facilities, including an *albergo* (hotel), tent pitches and water-sports centres, line the lake, overseen by the stone and stucco buildings of the upper older town, in whose castle Garibaldi made his headquarters.

3 Lodrone

The twin towns of Ponte Caffaro and Lodrone mark the boundary between Lombardy and the Trentino, where the architecture begins to show Alpine influences almost immediately. Over the bridge, a winding road (on the right) leads to **Troticoltura Armanini**, a trout and salmon farm. You can buy smoked fish, or just visit the rearing pools.

Open: Mon–Fri 8am–noon & 1.30–5.30pm, Sat 8am–noon.

Shortly after Darzo, turn right, following signs to Riva or Riva del Garda.

4 Storo

The old town clusters under a sheer cliff as the road winds past a rare public laundry basin, still in use. The road climbs quickly along a corniche before entering a narrow cleft that it shares with a rocky river. Watch out for a waterfall on the left; a trail leads down to it from a lay-by further up the road.

5 Passa Ampola

At 747m (2,450ft) altitude, the road enters a long green valley. A boardwalk provides access to the bird-rich, reedy, bio-reserve at Lago d'Ampola, called Biotopo. Rare lilies and aquatic plants grow in the reserve. At Tiarno di Sopra, just off the road to the left, brightly coloured houses, enclosed by stone walls with flower boxes, line the river bank.

6 Lago di Ledro

Tiny Lago di Ledro is overlooked by woody mini-parks with benches. In attractive Molina di Ledro, the **Museo delle Palafitte** displays Bronze Age artefacts dating back to the 2nd millennium BC. One of the dwellings from that period has been reconstructed. *Tel: (0464) 508 182. Open: daily mid-June–mid-Sept 10am–1pm & 2–6pm; mid-Sept–mid-June 9am–1pm & 2–5pm. Admission charge.*

7 Pre

The steep road descending from Molina di Ledro looks directly down onto the rooftops of Pre, whose hillsides are green with farms and vineyards. Pre is at the bottom of a valley so steep that from November to February its residents see neither sun nor moon.

A long tunnel leads almost directly into Riva del Garda, and the S-45b, which follows the lake shore back to Salò.

Tiny mountain towns overlook Lake Idro

Excursion: Rovereto

Less than 25km (16 miles) from the northern end of Lake Garda, Rovereto is a city packed with history. Dinosaurs lived here and left their footprints in mud that solidified to rock, preserving the prints intact. Jump ahead to the 20th century, and this area witnessed some of the bitterest World War I campaigns. In between these times, castles were built, churches decorated, vineyards planted, and the results of this all combine to make Rovereto and its environs a fascinating destination.

Castello di Rovereto

Crowning the city, this 13th-century fortress looks over the red-roofed town to steep mountains that enclose the Adige Valley. The museum gives a dramatic and poignant picture of the impact that World War I had on all of northern Italy. The artefacts, photographs and posters are so graphic and well arranged that the story is clear in any language. Look through the racks of photographs showing the liberation of towns and compare nearby Riva del Garda then and now.
Via Castelbarco 7 (reach it from Piazza Podesta). Tel: (0464) 438 100; www.museodellaguerra.it. Open: July–Sept Tue–Fri 10am–6pm, Sat & Sun 9.30am–6.30pm; Oct–June Tue–Sun 10am–6pm. Admission charge.

Dinosaur tracks

Spread over the mountainside, south of town, are about 350 footprints of prehistoric creatures, dating back 200 million years. Along with distinct single foot imprints, there are entire paths of dinosaur tracks. The first of these is a 15-minute walk from the road, and the tracks continue for some distance. Well-illustrated signs help to interpret the tracks and the animals that left them.
Follow signs for the Ossario di Castel Dante, then follow Strada degli Artiglieri to the car park, clearly marked.

Strada degli Artiglieri

After seeing pictures in the castle museum, the memorials lining the road to the dinosaur tracks – and the name of the road itself – fall into place. In World War I, Italian soldiers dragged and pushed heavy artillery up this steep route, digging defensive positions into the mountainside. The memorials are to men lost here. Each evening Rovereto commemorates the thousands who died by ringing the huge bell named the **Maria Dolens**, cast from cannon contributed by both sides that fought in the war.

Villa Lagarina

Across the Adige, this tiny village calls itself the 'Little Salzburg', and there is a connection. The church of **Santa Maria Assunta** was created by the same artists that built Salzburg's cathedral. Their style is clear in the marble altar and elaborate Baroque stucco work. Although such Baroque interiors are common to the north, this is one of the few so far south.

Open: Mon–Sat 9am 1pm & 3–5pm, Sun during service.

Vini Vallagarina

Wineries are dotted around the valley surrounding Rovereto, and there is an association of wineries that welcomes visitors to the tastings of a number of local varieties. All the wines there are for sale.

Via Brancolino 4, Nogaredo.
Tel: (0464) 412 073. Open: Mon–Fri 8am–noon & 2–6pm.

For more information visit www.infotrentino.com

Rovereto's impressive castle contains a museum of the world wars

Verona

In few cities do the Roman, medieval and Renaissance remain so distinct, yet blend so harmoniously as they do in this lovely city tucked into a sweeping 'S' curve of the Adige River.

Today's city centre, the heart of life for the Veronese, is exactly where it was when the Romans walked its streets. The pedestrianised area includes the old forum (parts of which are visible) and one of Italy's most charming, enclosed medieval/Renaissance squares, Piazza dei Signori. More medieval and Renaissance buildings line the streets, which pass through Roman and medieval gates to reach a castellated bridge and the well-preserved medieval Castelvecchio on the river. Reminders that this town was the pride of the Venetian empire are found in the gracefully arched windows and the winged lion of St Mark, perched on a

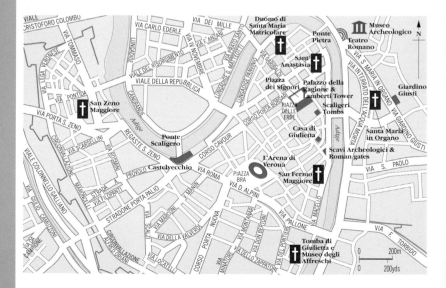

column surveying Piazza delle Erbe's morning market.

The area is easily explored on foot since most attractions are clustered together in the old city's walking streets. Via Mazzini connects Piazza Bra and the Roman arena to Piazza delle Erbe and, in the other direction, Via Roma leads to Castelvecchio and the river.

Verona is on the main Milan–Venice train line, and just north of the A-4 *autostrada*. Catullo Airport is in Villafranca, about 10km (6 miles) southwest, en route to Mantova. Shuttles run every 20 minutes between the airport and the railway station at Porta Nova. *Tel: (045) 805 7911. Operates: 6am–11.30pm.*

Although most central streets are closed to traffic, hotel guests may enter to unload luggage. Metered parking can be found along the river on Lungadige Capuleti, near Ponte Aleardi bridge. A 24-hour car park is just south of Piazza Bra, at Piazza Cittadella. Some hotels have spaces reserved for clients.

Via Mazzini connects Piazza Bra and Piazza delle Erbe

THE ORIGINAL ROMEO AND JULIET STORY

Luigi da Porto, a writer from Vicenza, borrowed the names of two local families when he wrote the original version of *Romeo and Juliet*, but it was William Shakespeare who made audiences take the characters to heart. In fact, they – or at least Juliet – take on a life of their own as Verona's number one tourist attraction. The entirely fictional story is set in Verona, and the city at first humoured tourists by assigning Juliet a medieval 'home' and even adding an appropriate balcony in the 1930s. A more recent addition is a tomb for the heroine. Romeo is largely ignored, although a fine medieval house opposite the della Scala tombs has been assigned to him.

To use a bus, buy a ticket before boarding from a newsstand or tobacco shop. Inexpensive daily tourist tickets are available, and a VeronaCard (buy at newsstands or participating attractions) combines museum admissions with bus transport. Taxi ranks are at Piazza Bra, Porto Nuovo (railway station), Piazza delle Erbe and Piazza San Zeno; cabs are metered. Radio-dispatched taxis: *Tel: (045) 532 666. IAT Verona, Via Alpini 9, off Piazza Bra. Tel: (045) 806 8680; fax: (045) 800 3638; email: iatverona@provinciavr.it. www.tourism.verona.it*

L'Arena di Verona

For almost two millennia, the arena has been a focal point in Verona. Since AD 30 it has served as a field for gladiators, a place of refuge from barbarian invasions and, from 1913, the venue for one of Europe's foremost opera festivals, the Stagione Lirica dell'Arena di Verona. With a seating capacity of about 22,000, Verona's arena is the third largest and best preserved in Italy, with only a portion of its outer ring missing. The arena forms one side of **Piazza Bra**, social centre of the Veronese. A phalanx of cafés in a row of 19th-century buildings forms another side of the *piazza*, and the 14th-century **Palazzo della Gran Guardia** adjoins the arched **Portoni della Bra** gate on the south side. This is where the Veronese begin their evening stroll, walking past the busy cafés and along fashionable Via Mazzini.
Piazza Bra. Open: daily 9am–6pm, on opera days 10am–3pm. Admission charge.

Casa di Giulietta

Through the efforts of a few romantics and, we suspect, many promoters, a fine medieval building with a balcony (added in the 1930s) came to be the 'home' of fictional Juliet from *Romeo and Juliet*, and is now a mecca for hordes of tourists. The walls leading into the small courtyard have literally been covered with graffiti, and the breast of the bronze statue of the charming heroine is burnished from the touching of thousands of hands.
Via Cappello 23. Tel: (045) 803 4303. Open: Tue–Sun 8.30am–7.30pm, Mon 1.30–7.30pm. Free admission to courtyard, charge to enter house.

Castelvecchio and Ponte Scaligero

Cangrande II della Seala built this impressive brick castle along the River Adige between 1355 and 1375 to secure his family's rule over the city. He connected it to the opposite bank with the **Ponte Scaligero**, castellated to make the bridge defensible. The castle, later an officers' mess for the Italian army, today houses one of Italy's premier art museums, with works by Bellini, Pisano, Francheschi, Rubens, Falconetti, Montagna, Tintoretto, Tiepolo and Guardi. Walking from room to room takes you through a history of Italian secular and religious art from the 13th through to the 19th centuries, with most artefacts originating from palaces, churches and monasteries in Verona and its province.

Corso Castelvecchio (end of Corso Cavour). Tel: (045) 594 734. Open: Tue–Sun 9am–7pm, last entry 6pm. Admission charge.

Duomo di Santa Maria Matricolare

Verona's cathedral is a fine example of the blending of architectural styles. On the site of a Roman temple and later a 5th-century Christian church, the present church was begun in 1139. In the centuries it took to complete, Romanesque, Gothic and Renaissance styles of architecture washed over Italy and were incorporated in the cathedral. The two-storey Romanesque portal is by medieval sculptor Nicolo, and Titian's 1530 painting of the Assumption is located in the first chapel to the left. The choir screen is the work of Michele Sanmicheli (1484–1559), who designed many of Verona's palaces and reworked the city defences.

L'Arena di Verona is the city's most recognisable landmark

Piazza Duomo. Tel: (045) 592 813.
Open: Mar–Oct Mon–Sat
10am–5.30pm, Sun 1.30–5.30pm;
Nov–Feb Tue–Sat 10am–1pm &
1.30–4pm, Sun 1–5pm. Admission
charge.

Giardino Giusti

Nestled into the steep-sided hills of the
city on the east side of the River Adige,
the Giusti Gardens provide a cool place
to walk, rest or picnic. Designed and
built during the 15th and 16th
centuries, they are a fine example of
Renaissance landscape architecture.
Formal parterres of clipped hedges,
walkways, cypress trees and grottoes
occupy the lower level, and stepped
pathways lead upwards to views over
the garden.
Via Giardino Giusti 2.
Tel: (045) 803 4029. Open: daily
Apr–Sept 9am–8pm; Oct–Mar
9am–sunset. Admission charge.

Palazzo della Ragione and Lamberti Tower

The 84m (276ft) Lamberti Tower rises
above the east side of Piazza delle Erbe,
easily identified by its striped layers of
pink brick and white tufa. It is part of
the medieval Palazzo della Ragione,
which has served as law courts for
centuries. Walk through the archway
and around into its courtyard for a view
of the Renaissance stairway that leads to
the upper levels. The tower, with
splendid views of the Dolomites on
clear days, is accessible by lift or stairs.

Giardino Giusti

Piazza dei Signori. Open: Mon–Thur
1.30–8.30pm, Fri–Sat 8.30am–10pm
(until midnight June–mid-Sept).
Admission charge.

Piazza delle Erbe

The long, narrow shape of Piazza delle
Erbe hints at its one-time role as the
Roman Hippodrome. Medieval
buildings, some with fine frescoes on
their outer walls, line its edges. Almost
from the beginning, this space has served
as an important marketplace. The Roman
statue in the centre, the **Madonna of
Verona**, acquired this role only in 1368.
The lion of Saint Mark, on its column at
one end, was erected during Venetian
rule, and the **Palazzo Maffei** just behind
it dates from the 17th century. Excavated
remnants of the Roman temple of
Jupiter are visible inside.

Piazza dei Signori

One of the loveliest in the city, this *piazza* is surrounded by the palaces of Verona's medieval rulers, the della Scala family. In the centre is an 1865 statue of Dante Alighieri, who took refuge in Verona during his exile from Florence. Along one side of the *piazza* is the **Loggia del Consiglio** with frescoes and statues of local notables. Look on the palace wall for the denunciation box where medieval Veronese could get rid of a rival by dropping a discreet note to the duke.

San Fermo Maggiore

In the 11th century, the old church became the crypt of the Benedictines' new church. It changed again in 1260 when the Franciscans added the Gothic pink brick and white tufa façade, but throughout all the renovations the crypt remained little changed, retaining 7th- and 8th-century frescoes. The marble pulpit dates from 1396, the work of Antonio da Mestre.

Stradone San Fermo. Tel: (045) 592 813. Open: Mar–Oct Mon–Sat 10am–6pm, Sun 1–6pm. Shorter hours in winter. Free admission.

Scaligeri tombs

Adjoining Piazza dei Signori, the small elegant church of **Santa Maria Antica**, consecrated in 1185, was the family church of the della Scala family and it was here that they were laid to rest. The two tombs with mounted warriors

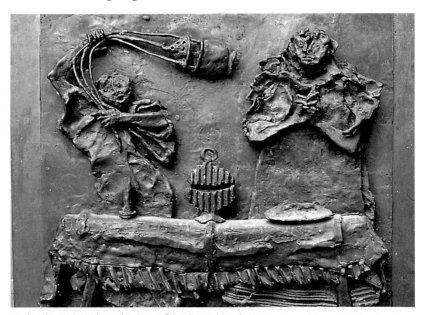

Modern bronze panels on the doors of San Fermo Maggiore

Courtyard of Tomba di Giulietta

are of Cansignorio, who died in 1375, and Mastino II, who died in 1351. The former was designed by Bonino da Campione and the latter was sculpted by Giovanni di Rigino.
Via Arche Scaligeri, off Piazza dei Signori. Open: tombs always visible. Church open: daily 7.30am–12.30pm & 3–7pm. Admission charge.

San Zeno Maggiore

Named after the first Bishop of Verona, and last rebuilt between 1123 and 1135, San Zeno is considered one of Europe's finest examples of Romanesque architecture. The 12-section rose window, attributed to Brioloto, dates from the 8th century. The triumph of medieval artistry, in a church replete with it, may be the 11th- and 12th-century bronze panels on the front doors. The left panels, the oldest, depict the life of Christ. On the right there are Old Testament events and

two miracles of San Zeno, whose remains rest in the glass-enclosed coffin in the crypt. The wooden, polychromed ceiling of the nave dates from 1386, and Andrea Mantegna's most celebrated triptych, painted in 1457, is on the main altar. The adjoining cloisters are Romanesque and Gothic.
Piazza San Zeno. Tel: (045) 592 813. Open: Mar–Oct Mon–Sat 8.30am–6pm, Sun 1–6pm. Shorter hours Nov–Feb. Admission charge.

Sant'Anastasia

It took from 1290 until the 15th century to complete this church, and even then the façade was never finished. Just inside the entrance is a pair of very unusual holy water fonts; the one on the left is called *Gobbo* (Humpback) and was sculpted by Gabriele Caliari, father of artist Paolo Veronese, in 1495. Near the Pellegrini chapel is the restored fresco *St George and the Princess*, which was painted by Pisanello in 1438.

Piazza Sant'Anastasia. Tel: (045) 592 813. Open: Mar–Oct Mon–Sat 9am–6pm, Sun 1–6pm; Nov–Feb Tue–Sat 10am–1pm & 1.30–7pm, Sun 1–5pm. Admission charge.

Santa Maria in Organo

Built in the 15th century, this church contains outstanding inlaid wood marquetry, the work of Fra Giovanni da Verona in the late 1400s. Decorating the choir stalls, lectern and sacristy, the inlay simulates everyday things. Shelves and display cupboards are an illusion, as are the lifelike chickens and rabbits.

Piazza Isolo, Via San Chiara. Open: daily 9am–noon & 3–6pm. Free admission.

Teatro Romano and Museo Archeologico

Still used today, the 1st-century BC Roman theatre has much of its original seating, but the performance areas are contemporary. Shakespeare plays and other drama are staged here, as well as classical music, jazz and ballet. The theatre overlooks the five-arch span of Ponte Pietra, a Roman bridge rebuilt after its destruction in World War II. Above the theatre seats is a small museum of Roman artefacts, especially stone-carved architectural details.

Regaste Redentore 2. Tel: (045) 800 0360. Open: Tue–Sun 8.30am–7.30pm, Mon

1.30–7.30pm. Closed: performance nights. Admission charge.

Scavi Archeologici and Roman gates

The Scavi are the archaeological digs that have brought Verona's Roman past back into view. Look on Via Cappello, off Piazza delle Erbe, for foundations and a well-preserved Roman city gate, **Porta Leoni**. The remains of the gate tower are below street level.

Tomba di Giulietta e Museo degli Affreschi

Even fictional heroines must have tombs. This ancient stone sarcophagus is empty but atmospheric. It is in a former convent that has become a small museum of fresco art. Be prepared for more of the Romeo and Juliet cult excesses.

Via Shakespeare (off Via del Pontiere). Tel: (045) 800 0361. Open: Tue–Sun 8.30am–7.30pm, Mon 1.30–7.30pm. Admission charge.

Porta Borsari, one of the Roman gates

Verona

Walk: Old Verona

With many of its prime sights so close, and connected by pedestrianised streets, the best way to see Verona is by walking. Cafés and restaurants are well placed, offering plenty of opportunity to rest en route.

Although the walk could easily take two days with stops to tour each attraction and the museum at Castelvecchio, the walking time is about 2 hours.

Begin at Piazza Bra.

1 L'Arena di Verona

A good vantage point from which to contemplate the arena is a café on the north side of Piazza Bra.
Follow Via degli Alpini east along the south side of Piazza Bra, turning left at Via Maffei, which becomes Stradone San Fermo, to reach San Fermo Maggiore.

2 San Fermo Maggiore

The church is on the right (*see p137*).
Continue past the church, turning left on Via Leoni. Porta Leoni is on the left.

3 Porta Leoni

Excavations in the street show the base of a tower, and on the left is a Roman gate, which was hidden for centuries after being incorporated into a building. Beyond is the courtyard of the so-called **Casa di Giulietta**.
Continue on Via Cappello to Piazza delle Erbe.

4 Piazza delle Erbe

This ancient market square is usually filled with the umbrellas of vendors

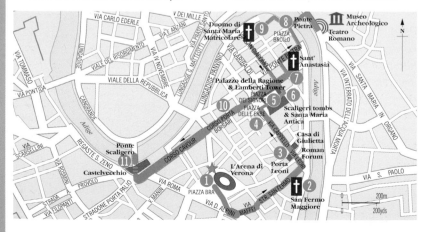

selling snacks, souvenirs and fresh produce. Notice the frescoes on the buildings along the side. Above is the **Lamberti Tower**.

Follow the passageway under the Lamberti Tower that leads to Piazza dei Signori.

5 Piazza dei Signori

Opposite the statue of Dante is the entrance to the Palazzo della Ragione and the Lamberti Tower.

From Piazza dei Signori go through the arch at the north end of the square.

6 Scaligeri tombs and Santa Maria Antica

On your right, the church of Santa Maria Antica and tombs (*see pp137–8*) are off a tiny *piazza*.

Past the tombs turn left and continue to Corso Sant'Anastasia, taking it to the right.

7 Sant'Anastasia

As well as this church (*see pp138–9*), a 15th-century palace faces onto the small *piazza*. This is now the Hotel Due Torri.

Leaving the church, cross the piazza *and turn right on Via Massalongo, following it one block and turning right on Via Ponte Pietra. Follow it to a small square, bearing left to reach the bridge.*

8 Ponte Pietra and Teatro Romano

There is a good view of the theatre from the bridge. In the theatre is the Museo Archeologico (*see p139*).

Retrace your route across the bridge and turn right into Piazza Broilo, bearing left to reach the back of the Duomo.

9 Duomo

Behind the Duomo is the small 8th-century church of San Giovanni in Fonte.

Leaving the Duomo, walk straight ahead to Via San Giacomo, turning left and following it to Corso Sant'Anastasia. Turn right, returning to Piazza delle Erbe, where the street becomes Corso Porta Borsari.

10 Corso Porta Borsari

This was the main street of Roman Verona, and you will pass through the 1st-century Roman gate, **Porta Borsari**. Further on, the 1st-century Roman **Arco dei Gavi**, along the river, was moved here complete with the stone pavement bearing chariot tracks.

Here the street name changes to Corso Cavour.

11 Castelvecchio and Ponte Scaligero

The castle is on the right and beyond it is the bridge.

Opposite the castle gate, Via Roma returns you to your starting point at Piazza Bra.

The Madonna di Verona in Piazza delle Erbe

Walk: Old Verona

Excursion:
The Valpolicella region

The mountainous landscape surrounding the deep-cut valleys of the Fumane, Negrar and Marano rivers north of Verona is home to some of Italy's most popular wines. Among the vineyards are villas, prehistoric sites, extraordinary fossils and a host of natural attractions.

Wine aficionados can sample the product at both modest little operations and wineries whose names are recognised all over the world. Pedemonte is a good base

for exploring (*see pp170–71*).
Ufficio Turistico Valpolicella, Viale Ingelheim 7, San Pietro in Cariano. Tel/fax: (045) 770 1920.

Museo Preistorico e Paleontologico

Palaeontology and prehistory are so much a part of this fossil-laden region that this museum is a good starting place. Along with a 70-million-year-old 7m (23ft) long shark, the museum has an astonishing collection of artefacts of local prehistoric peoples.
Piazza della Bona, Sant'Anna d'Alfaedo. Tel: (045) 532 656; www.lessiniamusei.it. Informa Parco (information centre), Via Amfiteatro 10. Tel: (045) 801 4987. Open: mid-May–mid-Sept Tue–Sun 9.30am–12.30pm & 3.30–6.30pm; mid-Sept–mid-May Wed, Sat & Sun 10am–noon & 3–5pm. Admission charge.

Parco delle Cascate di Molina

A whole series of waterfalls drops from the medieval village of Molina, in the

Fumane Valley. The route begins at the **Museo Botanico della Lessinia**, helpful in identifying the many indigenous plants in the park (*Tel: (045) 7720 145. Open: Apr–Sept daily 9am–7.30pm; Oct–Mar Sat & Sun 9.30am–4pm). Vivere Molina, Via Bacilieri 1. Tel: (045) 772 0185; www.parcodellecascate.it. Admission charge.*

Ponte di Veja

Follow the unnumbered road north from Negrar, through Fane, following signposts to Giare and Ponte di Veja. Europe's largest natural bridge, Ponte di Veja once formed the entry to a cave where prehistoric people lived. An aboriginal house is replicated at the park entrance. A short walk leads past the top and down under the arch, which is 29m (95ft) high, 6m (20ft) wide and spans a distance of 50m (164ft). Human artefacts from 100,000 years ago were found here. *Free admission.*

San Giorgio

Follow the unnumbered road north from Sant'Ambrogio di Valpolicella to San Giorgio. The church is at the top, in the village centre. The Longobard Romanesque church of **Pieve di San Giorgio**, and the town clustering around it atop a steep hill, are built from the stone that was carved away to flatten the hilltop. Behind the church is a gem of a cloister, tiny but perfectly proportioned, with some original carved capitals. Inside the church are rare 8th-century Longobard features.

Villa Mosconi-Bertani

It is a rare privilege to stand surrounded by frescoes in such near-perfect, original condition as those in the central hall of Villa Bertani. Built by a follower of Palladio, the neoclassical villa stands amid the vineyards it has made famous. Bertani's wines, among the most sought-after Valpolicella labels, are sold in a wing of the villa. Tastings include foods and a visit inside the villa, or tours are offered without tastings, both by prior booking. *Novare (Negrar). Tel: (045) 601 1211. Open: Mon–Fri 9am–noon & 2–6pm, Sat 9am–noon.*

Villa Rizzardi

The 18th-century villa, also a premier winery, has particularly fine Italianate and English gardens. Designed in the late 1700s by Luigi Trezza, the highlight is a garden amphitheatre enclosed by clipped hedges. *Via Verdi 4, Bardolino. Tel: (045) 721 0028; www.guerrieri-rizzardi.com. Open: Mon–Sat 10am–1pm & 3–7pm, Sun 10am–1pm.*

Cloister of Pieve di San Giorgio

Mantova

Surrounded on three sides by the Mincio River, which widens into a series of lakes here, Mantova (Mantua) is an elegant old city, and an easy one to visit. While it does not overwhelm with its number of sights, it offers one extravaganza – a palace of several hundred rooms, decorated by some of the Renaissance's greatest artists.

IAT Ufficio Informazioni, Piazza Mantegna 6. Tel: (0376) 432 432; www.turismo.mantova.it; email info@turismo.mantova.it. Open: Mon–Sat 9am–12.30pm & 2–6pm, Sun 9am–12.30pm.

Basilica di San'Andrea

With the building of this church in 1472, architect Leon Battista Alberti is said to have brought the Renaissance to Mantua. The interior is Baroque in flavour, with coffered vaulted ceilings and an 80m (262ft) high dome. In the first chapel on the left, among paintings from his school, you will find the tomb of the artist Mantegna. Other highlights are a fine baptistery and the Strozzi tomb dating from 1529.
Piazza Mantegna.
Tel: (0376) 328 504.
Open: daily 7.30am–noon & 3–7pm.

Casa di Rigoletto

As with Juliet's house in Verona, this 15th-century house has little to do with Verdi's opera character, although a nice bronze statue in the garden brings him vividly to the scene. At one time, open-air performances of *Rigoletto* were performed here. It is

now home to the city's association of tour guides.
Behind the Duomo off Piazza Sordello.

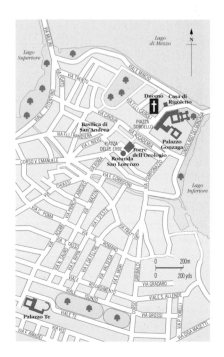

Torre dell'Orologio

Duomo

Opposite the Palazzo Ducale, the Baroque façade of the cathedral is matched by a fairly simple Baroque interior, all designed by Giulio Romano in the 16th century as a veneer to cover a Romanesque structure.

Piazza Sordello.
Tel: (0376) 320 220.
Open: daily 7am–noon & 3–7pm.

Palazzo Te

Once outside the city, Federico II Gonzaga's palace is now inside it. This excellent example of Renaissance Mannerism was designed by Giulio Romano in the 16th century as a place where Federico could meet up with his lover, Isabella Boschetti. The first-floor rooms are filled with exciting frescoes executed by Romano, a student of

THE GONZAGA FAMILY AND THEIR PALACE

The sprawling palace of the Gonzaga family dominates the Piazza Sordello much as the family dominated the city. The massive structure extends along one entire side of the *piazza* and for blocks behind it. Inside are more than 500 rooms, and outside there are extensive gardens.

The Gonzaga family came to power in 1328 when Luigi Gonzaga ousted the ruling Bonacolsi family, establishing a line that lasted until 1707. Luigi became Captain General and Imperial Vicar of the Holy Roman Empire, gaining the title of Marquess for the family. In 1530, the family was granted the Dukedom of Mantua in reward for the exceptional service that Francesco II had performed for the Holy Roman Empire in its struggle with Venice. In the mid-16th century, Ferrante Gonzaga, a military leader, was responsible for the enlargement of Castello Sforzesco in Milan. Great soldiers and strong rulers, the Gonzaga were also patrons of the arts, enhancing Mantova and their own palace by commissioning works by talented artists. The marriage of Isabella d'Este to Francesco II accelerated the family's patronage of the arts. The 16th-century saint Aloysius Gonzaga, who gave up his rights of inheritance to become a Jesuit, died while ministering to plague victims on the eve of his ordination.

Starting with the palace they had wrested from the Bonacolsi, the Gonzaga began a steady building process that eventually covered much of ancient Mantua. Room after room, garden after garden, the palace grew, and the finest artists and artisans were engaged to beautify it. Pisanello was brought in to decorate a room with paintings of medieval court life. Thought to be lost, these were rediscovered in 1972. In the Sala degli Specchi (Hall of Mirrors) the very first operas were performed by Claudio Monteverdi. In one room hang nine Flemish tapestries based on drawings by Raphael, and in the Apartment of the Metamorphoses the walls were decorated by Giulio Romano. The Apartment of Dwarfs is exquisitely crafted, but to the scale of 1m (3ft) adults.

In 1390 the family built the large Castello San Giorgio to control the adjacent waterways, and in 1470 Ludovico II adapted the castle as his residence. Inside, in the Camera degli Sposi (Newly-weds' Room), are frescoes by Mantegna. *Piazza Sordello. Tel: (0376) 382 150. Open: Tue–Sun 9am–6.30pm, last admission 5.30pm. Admission charge.*

Raphael. The Sala di Psiche (Psyche's Room) is exceptional, with themes of bacchanalian excess, as is the Sala dei Giganti with its towering giants and falling columns. Two museums are now housed in the *palazzo*: the Averbi collection of Egyptian artefacts and the Mondadori Fund collections of 19th-century and later paintings.
Viale Te.
Tel: (0376) 323 266.
Open: Mon 1–6pm, Tue–Sun 9am–6pm. Admission charge.

Rotonda San Lorenzo

This little 11th-century church was lost and presumed destroyed until the buildings that had surrounded it were taken down in 1908. The oldest church in the city, it is now restored. Its circular interior has an inner ring of Romanesque columns supporting a women's gallery (in early churches women were not allowed in the main part of the church, but a balcony was often added for them), and the walls bear remnants of 12th- and 13th-century

Mantua's main square, Piazza delle Erbe

Byzantine school frescoes. The *piazza* outside is a popular meeting place, the scene of the Thursday market, and many festivals are held here. Be sure to notice the magnificent terracotta façade on the Palazzo della Ragione diagonally in front of the Rotonda.

Piazza delle Erbe. Open: daily 10am–noon & 2.30–4.30pm.

Torre dell'Orologio

Another charming feature of Piazza delle Erbe is the 1473 astrological clock, situated in a tower topped with a small temple. The tower is attached to the 13th-century **Palazzo della Ragione** by a covered stairway that leads to an upper chamber. The chamber, which is open only for exhibitions, has excellent 13th-century frescoes.

The Risorgimento and the Red Cross

The Second War of Italian Independence in 1859 pitted Austria, as the occupying power in Lombardy, against the French and their allies, a Sardinian-Piedmontese force led by Vittorio Emanuele II. The Austrian army was defeated at Magenta on 4 June 1859 and withdrew to the east. It was unaware that its opponents, who themselves had no idea of the whereabouts of the Austrians, were moving in the same direction.

The sides were fairly evenly matched in number, comprising almost 250,000 men in all. Early on 24 June 1859, the rearguard of the

La Cappella Ossario

Austrians and the advance guard of the Franco-Italian forces met and clashed in the plains at the foot of the hills that rise at Solferino. Each army was uncertain of the numbers or positions of the other, and they fought in bloody and furious engagements throughout the day. In the evening, the Franco-Italian force broke through the Austrian lines and the latter began to withdraw.

In that one-day battle, the Austrians lost 14,000 killed or wounded and 8,000 missing or taken prisoner. Of the French and Piedmontese, there were 15,000 killed or wounded and 2,000 missing or captured. Dead and wounded men littered the fields of Solferino and there was no one to bury the former or to care for the latter. Neither side made any significant effort to help those who had become casualites in the fighting. The cost of the battle was so high that Emperor Napoleon III called for a conference at Villafranca, which resulted in a truce between the two forces.

Another consequence of the battle, however, was of more lasting significance to the whole world. A Swiss citizen, Jean-Henri Dunant,

Wall of nations at the Red Cross Monument

was appalled by the suffering of the wounded left lying unattended at Solferino. He organised emergency medical assistance for the wounded, and a group of people to bury the dead. In 1862, Dunant wrote his memoirs, *Un Souvenir de Solferino*, about the battle and its aftermath. In it he proposed that all countries join to form an emergency relief organisation. The first of these began in 1864, rapidly expanding to other countries around the globe.

Solferino was the birthplace of the International Red Cross and its Muslim equivalent, the Red Crescent. On a hillside in Solferino stands the solemn **Cappella Ossario**, a monument to the dead and an icon to the wastefulness of war. Behind the altar, thousands of skulls from the fallen look down upon those who come and pray. Below the chapel, the **Museo Storico** is a

memorial to those killed in the cause of Italian independence, containing material on the battle of Solferino. *Piazza Ossario, Solferino. Tel: (0376) 854 019. Both open: Tue–Sun 9am–noon. Ossario: free admission. Museo: admission charge.*

On the hill above Solferino, the **Memoriale della Croce Rossa**, which commemorates Dunant and the Red Cross, is a simple promenade of trees with a monument at the end. Beside the monument is a wall of stone plaques upon which are carved the names of all nations that participate in the Red Cross's voluntary humanitarian work. The monument and its grounds were fully restored in 2003 by Austrian volunteers. Standing guard above it all is the **Rocca di Solferino**, a stone tower built in 1022 and used by the Italian forces as an observation point.

Driving tour:
Along the Mincio River

The Mincio is not a very long river, flowing only a distance of about 50km (30 miles) as the crow flies, on its way from Lake Garda to join the Po south of Mantova. Parklands follow its banks, some of which are also nature reserves that protect the wetlands nourished by the river. No road follows the meandering waters far, but several country roads cross it.

Allow 1½ hours' driving time.

Begin at Peschiera, on the southern shore of Lake Garda.

1 Peschiera del Garda

The Mincio River flows out of Lake Garda, past the fortifications that guarded this important port (*see p125*). *Leave Peschiera on Via Secolo over the railway line, then go straight across the intersection onto Via Salvi and continue south, following signs to Ponti sul Mincio. Stay on the same road through*

Ponti and do not cross the river in Monzambano, but continue south, following signs towards Volta Mantovana. After about 3km (2 miles), turn left (east) at the crossing signposted to Valeggio. On arriving in Borghetto, turn right, then right again before the bridge.

2 Borghetto

Once devoted to silk manufacture, which harnessed the rushing Mincio

to power its mills, the village was abandoned when the mills closed. Yet recent restoration has given the village new life. Cafés and craft studios fill the buildings that sit picturesquely overlooking the water. As a backdrop, crossing the wide river is the impressive old fortified **Ponte Visconteo**. Guarding the entrance to Valeggio since 1393, its upper arches now stand in romantic partial ruin.

Carry on over the Ponte Visconteo, turning left at the end, then go right, following signs to Valeggio and the castle.

3 Valeggio

Castello Scaligeri overlooks the bridge, as well as the town below. On clear days you can see sweeping views north

Ponte Visconteo at Borghetto

to the Dolomites. *Castle open: daily during daylight hours. Tower open: Sun & holidays 9am–noon & 2.30–7pm. Admission charge to tower.*

In the valley below is **Parco Giardino Sigurtà**, in the former grounds of a villa that was commandeered by Napoleon as his headquarters. Now a park of 50 hectares (124 acres) it is so expertly landscaped into flower, topiary, herb and water gardens that it has been listed among the most beautiful gardens in the world. View it on foot, or by bicycle, rented golf cart or a 7km (4-mile) train line. *Tel: (0456) 371 033; www.sigurta.it. Open: daily Mar–Nov 9am–6pm. Admission charge.*

Saturday is market day in Valeggio, and an antiques market is held on the fourth Sunday of each month. *Turismo. Tel: (0457) 951 880; www.valeggio.com. For restaurants: www.info-valeggio.it. Go south on S-249, through Roverbella until its intersection with S-62, where you turn right, following signs to Mantova.*

4 Mantova

The Mincio widens into three lakes as it flows past Mantova. The area along the north shore, west of Mantova, is all part of the **Parco del Mincio**, and large stretches of the riverbank are protected as nature reserves. Excursion boats touring the three lakes are docked on the Viale Mincio, behind the palace.

Associazione Turistica Colline Moreniche del Garda, Piazza Torelli 1, Solferino. Tel: (0376) 854 360/001; www.collinemoreniche.it

Shopping

Think of shopping in Milan, and fashion immediately comes to mind. Although few can afford the showrooms of the Quadrilatero della Moda, these are prime streets for window shopping and good at sale time. Big-name designers are found on Via della Spiga, with eye-catching window displays and high prices. More affordable clothes are available from the shops along Corso Buenos Aires or Via Torino, aimed at a younger clientele. Even more budget-friendly are the shops that line Corso Vittorio Emanuele.

Most Milan stores open: Tue–Sat 9.30am–7.30pm, Mon 3.30–7.30pm. Smaller shops and those outside the centre open: Tue–Sat 9.30am–12.30pm & 3.30–7.30pm, Mon 3.30–7.30pm.

Accornero

Everything for the well-dressed home.
Via Ponte Vetro 17. Tel: (02) 8909 6297.

Battistoni

Men's shirts, with fragrance ironed in.
Via della Spiga 2. Tel: (02) 794 643.

Coin

Everyday items at everyday prices.
*Piazza Cinque Giornate.
Tel: (02) 5519 2083.*

La Rinascente

Moderately priced department store.
Piazza del Duomo. Tel: (02) 885 21.

Trussardi

Expensive leather accessories.
Via Sant'Andrea 5. Tel: (02) 7602 0380.

Discount designer outlets

Designer fashions can be found in outlets with 50 to 70 per cent off the retail price.

Bettina Stock

Discounts of 50 to 70 per cent.
*Via Simone d'Orsenigo 3.
Tel: (02) 5411 6292.*

Eivissa

Discounted leather goods and furs.
Viale Monza 38. Tel: (02) 284 7954.

I Santi

An outlet located at the factory.
*Via B Corio 2. Tel: (02) 5416 981.
Open: Mon–Fri 8.30am–12.30pm & 1.30–5.30pm. Metro: Porta Romana.*

Te'Con Amiche

Consignments and samples near Piazza San Babila.
*Via Visconti di Modrone 33.
Tel: (02) 7733 1506.*

Factory outlets

The area west of Lake Maggiore is famed for its factory outlets. More than 50 of these sell everything from high-end cooking utensils to skis.

Alessi

Cutting-edge design meets pure whimsy in the colourful showroom of the Alessi factory, where cookware and table accessories can be purchased at reduced prices.

Via privata Alessi, Crusinallo di Omegna. Tel: (0323) 868 648; www.alessi.com. Open: Mon–Sat 9.30am–6pm; Dec also Sun 9.30am–6pm.

Lagostina

The rows of discounted pots and pans and kitchen utensils are irresistible.

Parco Commerciale Laghi, Via Stampa 62, Gravellona Toce. Tel: (0323) 865 058. Open: 9am–7pm.

Pretti

Terry-cloth beach towels, robes and household items at bargain prices.

Viale Azari 94, Verbania-Pallanza. Tel: (0323) 556 939. Open: Wed–Sat 9.30am–12.30pm & 2–6.30pm, Mon & Tue 2–6.30pm. Closed: Sun.

Markets

Milan has a full schedule of street markets, listed in the free paper *Hello Milano* found at the tourist office. A Saturday-morning market is held at Viale Papiniano.

Crafts

Outdoor artisans' fairs offer unique original works at direct-from-the-artist prices. Artisans' studios are often found in lakeside resort towns and the mountain towns of the Valle d'Aosta are known for woodcrafts.

Les Amis du Bois

A cooperative of master woodcarvers.

Fraz. Villes Dessus 9, Introd (16 km/ 10 miles from Aosta). Tel: (0165) 955 57.

Vetroe

Stunning, original art glass.

Via Bersani 34, Orta San Giulio. Tel: (0322) 905 555.

Antiques

Serious collectors go to the antiquarians behind Sant'Ambrogio, while regular antiques markets are found at:

Como: last Saturday of each month.
Desenzano del Garda: first Sunday of each month except January and August.
Mantova: third Sunday of each month.
Milan: Naviglio Grande canal, last Sunday of each month.
Milan: Piazza Diaz (near Duomo), last Saturday of each month.
Milan: Via Fiori Chiari (Monte Napoleone), third Sunday of each month.
Verona: Piazza San Zeno, third Saturday of each month.

Como

Como is a major silk-manufacturing centre. Here you can buy scarves, shawls or neckties for low prices.

Martinetti

Silk manufacturer's retail outlet.

Via Torriani 41, Como. Tel: (031) 269 053. Open: Tue–Fri 8am–noon & 2.30–6pm, Mon 2.30–6pm, Sat 8am–noon.

Verona

Via Mazzini is the main street for chic shops, and these spread into the streets adjoining it. Around Verona and Lake Garda you will find colourful ceramics made in Nove de Bassano.

Entertainment

As the unquestioned entertainment capital of northern Italy, Milan has a busy calendar of everything from grand opera (see pp156–7) *and celebrity performances to avant-garde cinema and underground bands. The free* Hello Milano *publication, available at the tourist office, has a complete listing.*

Classical and semi-classical

Teatro Dal Verme
Concert theatre near Castello Sforzesco.
Via San Giovanni sul Muro 2.
Tel: (02) 2940 9724.

Sala Verdi, Conservatorio
Concert hall hosting well-known philharmonic orchestras.
Via Conservatorio 12.
Tel: (02) 6698 6956; www.soconcerti.it

Popular

Teatro Manzoni
A wide variety of musicians perform at this theatre.
Via Manzoni 42. Tel: (02) 7600 023.

Concert venues

Alcatraz
Leading Italian and European groups play here.
Via Valtellina 25. Tel: (02) 6901 6352.

FilaForum
Major venue for international stars – David Bowie, Placebo and the like.
Via G di Vittorio, Assago (shuttle bus from the Famagosta Metro station to the FilaForum in Assago).
Tel: (02) 5300 6501.

Magazzini Generali
Doubling as a dance club, this venue runs the gamut of music road shows.
Via Pietrasanta 14. Tel: (02) 5521 1313.

Clubs

As with hip clubs in any city, you need to know which night to go. The club that does disco on Tuesday may hip hop on Thursday, with a correspondingly different clientele. Some clubs won't let you past the door if you are not dressed smartly. They have their reputations to maintain as the places to see the *bella gente* ('beautiful people').

Many clubs use a card, punched for every drink, and then you pay as you leave. Admission charges may include one drink. All drinks – hard or soft – are usually the same price. Clubs don't get started until after midnight, closing around 4am. Most are closed in July and August.

Blue Note

Jazz soloists in an intimate setting.
Via Borsieri 37.
Tel: (02) 6901 6888.

Divina

Pure Milano-style décor and disco music.
Via Molino delle Armi at Via della Chiusa.
Tel: (02) 5843 1823.

G Lounge

Attracts a fashion-world clientele.
Via Larga 8
Tel: (02) 8053 042.

Gavi Café

The décor is entertainment enough.
Via Aselli 7.
Tel: (02) 7012 3136.

Jumpin' Jazz Ballroom

Traditional jazz for dancing, with live band.
Viale Monza 140 (upstairs).
Tel: (344) 3112 926.

La Banque

Popular venue with happy hour Friday.
Via Porrone 6.
Tel: (02) 8699 6565.

Plastic

Only the best-dressed (Milano style) will get through the door of this cool club.
Viale Umbria 120. Tel: (02) 733 996. Open:
Thur–Sat midnight–5am, Sun 8pm–2am. Closed: July–Aug.

Propaganda

Navigli district club with occasional live shows.
Via Castelbarco 11.
Tel: (02) 5831 0682.

Scimmie

A favourite in the Navigli; live shows are mostly blues and jazz.
Via Ascanio Sforza 49.
Tel: (02) 8940 2874.

Shocking Club

Arrive in time for the *apperitivi* hour and buffet, and stay for the good mix of music styles – and to see the fashion models that call it a home away-from-home. If you're not a student, skip Thursday.
Bastioni di Porta Nuova 12. Tel: (02) 6269 0045;
www.shockingclub.net.
Open: Tue & Thur–Sat.

Cinema

Cineteca, Spazio Oberdan

Regular programme of films in English.
Viale Vittorio Veneto 2.
Tel: (02) 7740 6300.

Festival del Film di Locarno

Outdoor film festival.
Piazza Grande, Locarno (Lake Maggiore). Open: mid-Aug.

Verona

Verona hosts a prestigious opera festival (*see pp156–7*) each summer.

Piazza dei Signori

Summer jazz.
Tel: (045) 806 6485;
www.comune.verona.it

Teatro Romano

Shakespeare, dance, concerts and ballet.
Regaste Redentore 2.
Tel: (045) 806 6485;
www.comune.verona.it

Teatro Dal Verme

Opera, opera everywhere

Opera may have a highbrow status elsewhere, but in Italy it still enjoys wide popularity. So wide, in fact, that arias are common background music in shops and it is not unusual to hear mobile phones ringing with the opening bars of *La Donna è Mobile*.

The first stop for any opera lover in Milan is La Scala and its museum. After major reconstruction and

Costume at La Scala museum

restoration, the great theatre now has not only a shining, clean face inside, but greatly enlarged and state-of-the-art backstage areas that will allow for even more elaborate productions. La Scala is more than just the performances to the Milanese, for whom it is also the centre of upper-crust social life.

Likewise, La Scala's museum has moved back to its permanent home adjoining the theatre, where it provides a memory-lane tour of the greatest performances and performers in opera history.

Verona's Roman arena is the scene of one of Europe's major opera festivals each summer, an annual event for more than 80 years. Five operas are performed in rotation from the end of June until the end of August in the open amphitheatre.

Nearly every Italian city of any size has a theatre where opera is performed, and many have resident companies. In addition to seeing opera performances, travellers in northern Italy can visit sights associated with operas and the composers who wrote them.

Composer Gaetano Donizetti was born in a very modest house at Via

Borgo Canale 14 in Bergamo, and, although his circumstances changed with the success of his music, he remained in his home town. The Museo Donizettiano, where many of his operas were written, is in his home (see p96). In Santa Maria Maggiore, the nearby basilica, his marble tomb has an honoured setting, and even now fresh flowers are still left there by grateful music lovers.

Giuseppe Verdi lived in Milan and died in the Hotel Grand et de Milan on Via Manzoni in 1901. As word of his fatal illness spread, people began to gather in silent vigil under his window, and straw was spread on the street below to quieten the sound of passing carriages. Verdi and his wife are buried in the **Casa di Riposo per Musicisti** (*Piazza Buonarroti 29*), a home for retired musicians that Verdi founded.

The region provided inspiration and settings, as well. Verdi composed *La Traviata* at Villa Margherita Ricordi in Cadenabbia, on Lake Como. Mantova was chosen as the setting for his opera *Rigoletto*, and a statue of the jester stands in a courtyard opposite the palace of the fictional duke who caused all the trouble. Gioacchino Rossini composed several arias inspired by the gardens at Villa Pliniana in Torno, where he was a house guest.

Arena di Verona
Piazza Bra 28, Verona. Tel: (045) 805 1811. Ticket sales: Via Dietro Anfiteatro 6/b. Tel: (045) 800 5151; fax: (045) 801 3287; www.arena.it

Rosetum
Opera, sometimes in concert format. *Via Pisanello 1, Milan. Tel: (02) 4009 2015.*

Teatro alla Scala
Piazza della Scala. Tel: (02) 805 3418; www.teatroallascala.org

Teatro Donizetti
Among the best-regarded opera houses in northern Italy, the Donizetti produces a full opera season, along with operetta and ballet seasons. *Piazza Cavour 15. Tel: (035) 416 0611; fax: (035) 416 0670; www.teatrodonizetti.it*

Statue of Rigoletto in Mantova

Children

Many of the things that Milan does best – shopping, art museums and historic churches – may leave children cold. However, they will warm to the lakes, especially Garda, with its perpetual holiday atmosphere.

Although not every place is suitable for all ages, the most child-friendly places in Milan are the armour collections at Castello Sforzesco (*see p27*) and Teatro delle Marionette (*Via Oglio 18. Tel: (02) 5521 1300*). Older children may enjoy the many working models in the Museo della Scienza e della Tecnica, although most signs are in Italian (*see pp35–6*) or the Duomo roof (*see p29*). When all else fails, head for one of Milan's many *gelato* counters.

Instead of trying to fit children into a Milan itinerary, it is better to make quick work of the city and head for more fertile ground. Castles are always a good bet, and there's a fine one as close as Angera (with a doll museum). The highest concentration of castles is in the Valtenesi, west of Lake Garda (*see p124*), although Malcesine and Sirmione have good ones, too.

Nearly every lake has either swinging cable cars or a creaking funicular to a mountain top: Mottorone at Stresa (*see p55*), Monte Baldo at Malcesine

(*see p118*), Monte San Salvatore at Lugano (*see p71*) and Brunate at Como (*see p82*). Older chidren will get a kick out of the quirky free transportation museum at Ranco, where they can walk under the tracks to see how a funicular works.

Boat rides on any of the lakes are a diversion, especially on the tiny boats that shuttle to islands: Isola Comacina (*see pp86–7*), Isola San Giulio (*see p67*), Monte Isola (*see pp104–5*) and the Borromean Islands (*see pp56–7*).

Natural wonders in the area are especially exciting for children because they involve cave people, dinosaurs and rivers doing amazing things. Cascata del Varone (*see p123*) and the Orrido di Bellano (*see p88*) are both chasms carved by waterfalls, Ponte di Veja is a huge natural arch where prehistoric people lived (*see p143*), and at Rovereto there are entire dinosaur tracks (*see p130*). Roman sites (*see pp12–13*), particularly those where gladiators fought, as they did in Verona's arena, are good for children old enough to have heard of the Romans (*see p134*).

Most towns have children's parks somewhere – Riva del Garda has a good one near the castle. Bright plastic slides and climbing jungles, swings, often little cars or even a mini-train, as in Aosta, provide a place to find playmates (children don't care if they don't speak the same language). Sometimes outdoor cafés will have a couple of plastic cars on springs to occupy young minds while parents relax with an espresso.

Festivals will always have children's activities and are colourful, lively

occasions with bands playing. Having a child with you is your ticket to join in the festivities instead of remaining an onlooker.

If you run out of distractions, consider the Hollywood-style amusement parks, the largest of which is Gardaland. This sprawls on forever, with plenty of rides and games. Don't go at weekends though, or you will spend most of your time in queues (*S-249, Castelnuovo del Garda. Tel: (045) 644 9777; www.gardaland.it*).

One last word: Don't be distressed when someone calls your son a *bimbo* – it means 'little boy'.

Como's children's amusement park

Sport and leisure

With all the water and mountains, there are sports for all interests. Tourist offices can provide information on instructors, sports centres and equipment rentals for nearly every sport, as well as hiking guides and maps.

Bungee jumping

If you seek mid-air thrills, head for the north end of Lake Garda.
Paolo Fazi, Lungolago Sabbioni, Riva. Tel: (0464) 520 822.

Football (soccer)

Milan is home to two top-flight football clubs that use the same stadium in the San Siro district.

AC Milan is the older club, having been founded in 1899, while **Inter** was formed in 1908. Rivalry between their fans is intense, and often neighbours won't speak to each other if they support opposing sides. Twice a year the teams clash in Serie A. *Stadio Giuseppe Meazza, Via Piccolomini 4. Tel: (02) 404 2432. It is best to get tickets at: AC Milan Point, Via San Gottardo 2, Piazza XXIV Maggio. Tel: (02) 8942 2711. Open: Mon–Sat 10am–7.30pm. Inter Ticket One/Spazio Oberdan, Viale Vittorio Veneto. Tel: (02) 2953 6577. Open: Tue–Sun 10am–9pm.*

Golf

Lombardy offers a wealth of opportunity for golfers, with 35 nine- or 18-hole courses, nine promotional courses and nine practice locations. Be sure to call for guest status and to reserve time. Most courses are open all year.

Lake Como: Golf Club Villa d'Este has an 18-hole course, among Europe's most challenging par 69 courses, 7km (4 miles) from Como. *Via per Cantù 13, Montorfano. Tel: (031) 200 200; www.villadeste.it. Open: Mar–Dec. Closed: Tue.*

Golf Club Menaggio e Cadenabbia, on the west side of the lake, is an 18-hole, par 70 course, 40km (25 miles) from Como. *Via Golf 12, Grandola ed Uniti. Tel: (0344) 321 03; www.menaggio.it. Open: Mar–Nov.*

Lake Garda: Arzaga Golf Club is an 18-hole par 72 course, southwest of the lake and 25km (15½ miles) from Brescia, 65km (40 miles) from Verona. *Carzago di Calvagese della Riviera.*

Sport and leisure

Tel: (030) 680 600; www.palazzoarzaga.com.
Gardagolf Country Club has three
nine-hole courses, par 35–6, 30km
(18½ miles) from Brescia, 65km (40
miles) from Verona. *Via Angelo Omodeo
2, Soiano del Lago. Tel: (0365) 674 707;
www.gardagolf.com. Closed: Mon.*
Lake Iseo: Franciacorta Golf Club, an
18-hole, par 72 course, 20km (12½
miles) west of Brescia. *Via Provinciale
34/B, Nigoline di Corta Franca. Tel: (030)
984 167. Closed: Sept–May Tue.*
Lake Lugano: Golf Club Lanzo is a
nine-hole, par 37 course, 16km

(10 miles) from Lugano and 30km
(18½ miles) from Como. *Località Piano
delle Noci, Lanzo d'Intelvi. Tel: (031) 839
060; www.golflombardia.it. Open:
Apr–Nov. Closed: Mon.*
Milan East: Molinetto Country Club
is an 18-hole, par 71 course, 10km
(6 miles) from Milan. *Strada Statale
Padana Superiore 11, Cernusco Sul
Naviglio. Tel: (0292) 105 128; email:
molinetto.c.c@ntt.it. Closed: Mon.*
Milan North: Golf Club Milano in
Monza has an 18-hole and a nine-hole
course, par 72–36, 18km (11 miles)

All the lakes have plenty of boat rental opportunities

from Milan. *Via Mulini San Giorgio 7, Parco di Monza. Tel: (039) 303 081; www.golfclubmilano.it. Closed: Mon.*
Milan South: Golf Club Le Rovedine, 18 holes, par 72, only 4km (2¹/₂ miles) from Milan. *Via Karl Marx 18, Noverasco di Opera. Tel: (0257) 606 420; www.rovedine.com. Closed: Mon.*
Milan West: Golf Green Club Lainate, 18 holes, par 71, 10km (6 miles) from Milan. *Via A Manzoni 45, Lainate. Tel: (0293) 708 69; www.golf-hotel.it*

Horse riding
Centro Ippico Tenuta la Torre takes you out into the hills and mountains around Lake Como, welcoming all levels of expertise and with English-speaking guides (*Tel: (0348) 894 7814/008 0869. Yellow signs between Menaggio and Porlezza. Bus: line C12*). At the south end of the lake, near Como, you can ride from a 13th-century farm in the fields and woods around tiny Lake Montorfano with **Circolo Ippico Il Grillo** (*Via Chigollo 7, Capiago Intimiano. Tel: (031) 462 219*). Itineraries run from an hour to a full day, and at all levels of difficulty. English and Western saddles are available at both places.

Mountain biking
With so many mountains, there is a lot of territory to explore. At the northern end of Lake Garda, **Nautic Club Riva** has a team of guides and instructors for riders of all levels. Tours are half- or full-day (*Viale Rovereto 44, Riva.*

Tel: (0464) 552 453; www.nauticclubriva.com). **Marco Segnana Surf Centre** also has mountain bike rentals (*Foci del Sarca, Torbole and Lungolago dei Pini 19, Riva. Tel: (0464) 505 963; www.surfsegnana.it*), as does **Carpentari Bike Shop** (*Via Matteotti 16, Torbole. Tel: (0464) 505 500; www.carpentari.com*). On Lake Como, rent from **Cavalcario Club** (*Guello di Bellagio. Tel: (031) 964 814*).

Sailing and boating
On all but the smallest lakes you will find plenty of rental boats of all varieties. Ask for *barca* (boat), *barca a vela* (sailing boat) or *motoscafo* (motorboat). Put these together with *noleggio* (for hire) and you will be on the water before you know it. Because of the predictable winds, the northern end of Lake Garda is among one of the best places to sail. **Nautic Club Riva** rents catamarans and sailing boats, and its instructors can teach both beginners and advanced sailors (*Viale Rovereto 44, Riva. Tel: (0464) 552 453; www.nauticclubriva.com*).

Canoeists on the northern end of Lake Garda should go to **Paolo Fazi** at Lungolago Sabbioni for hourly, half-day and full-day rentals of single and double boats (*Tel: (0464) 520 822*).

Swimming
Along all the lakes look for small *piscina* (pool) or *spiaggia* (beach) signs. Don't expect broad sandy beaches –

most are stony or made of gravel, so you will need a blanket or heavy towel. Many cities and towns have swimming pools that are open to visitors as well as to locals. In Riva, you can choose between **Piscina Enrico Meroni** (*Via Martini 25. Tel: (0464) 520 078*) and **Riva Sport Centre** (*Viale dei Tigli 40. Tel: (0464) 552 072. Admission charge*).

Windsurfing

Some of Europe's prime windsurfing waters are at the northern end of Lake Garda. Light winds in the mornings and stronger afternoon winds provide varied challenges, especially good for learners. **Nautic Club Riva** has qualified instructors and rental equipment (*Viale Rovereto 44, Riva. Tel: (0464) 552 453; www.nauticclubriva.com*). Waters off Torbole, just a few kilometres from Riva, are the best.

Marco Segnana Surf Centre is a large and professional facility with instruction and rental on a beautiful beach (*Foci del Sarca, Torbole and Lungolago dei Pini 19, Riva. Tel: (0464) 505 963; www.surfsegnana.it*).

Cycling in the Gran Paradiso National Park, Valle d'Aosta

Food and drink

Milan is known for its excellent restaurants, largely because the Milanese often dine out, and demand quality. Fashionable city hot spots and some restaurants around the lakes can be expensive, but you will find reasonably priced restaurants everywhere.

That is not to suggest that you should avoid the dining establishments, often in villa hotels, where creative chefs have gained a name for themselves. These restaurants offer a chance to sample the artistry of some of Europe's finest chefs, and it would be a shame to miss out on such an experience. You will need to book well ahead for any of these, especially on a weekend. For those in villas, it is often more economical to book a room with dinner (*see pp176–7*).

A *trattoria* usually has a more limited menu and lower prices than a *ristorante* (both words mean 'restaurant'), and frequently the waiter will describe the day's specials in place of a menu. An *osteria* is a wine bar that serves snacks and sometimes a few dishes. A *pizzeria* is normally a restaurant that specialises in wood-oven pizzas. That said, the terms are used interchangeably and a *trattoria* may be fancier and pricier than the *ristorante* next door, and the *osteria* may be a chichi, countrified inn.

If in doubt, ask to see a menu (generally posted at the door). For home-style cooking, look for signs advertising *cucina casalinga*. For a sandwich, go to a bar or café.

A typical meal includes a *primo* (first course) of *pasta* (pasta) or *risotto* (rice). A *secondo* (main course) often includes only the meat or fish, and perhaps a small serving of vegetables. Vegetables (*contorni*) and salads (*insalate*) are usually ordered separately. *Dolci* (sweets) follow. *Antipasti* are small dishes that precede the pasta course. Although Italians may progress through all these courses, this does not mean you need to. Ask about the size of the pasta serving to determine how many courses to order, since handmade *ravioli* tends to be far lighter than a *penne* or *linguini* dish.

If breakfast (*colazione*) is not included in the accommodation price, cafés are better value than hotels. Coffee with hot milk – *cappuccino* or *caffè latte* – is drunk only at breakfast.

Coffee ordered at any other time of day should be *espresso*, although waiters will automatically assume tourists want *caffè americano*.

REGIONAL DISHES

Milan's speciality dishes are *cotoletta milanese* (veal cutlet) and *risotto*, a creamy rice dish incorporating anything from porcini mushrooms to seafood. On the lakes and in Verona, *polenta* is a favourite – a maize porridge often served with porcini. *Ossobuco*, braised veal shins, is a heartier rustic dish. Lake fish are abundant, usually grilled or pan-fried. Vegetables fresh from nearby farms are used in season, so you may find every restaurant offering artichokes or asparagus at the same time.

RESTAURANTS

Hours are generally noon to 2.30pm or 3pm, and 7pm to 10pm or later. Italians usually arrive after 8pm. Most restaurants in Milan close for the whole month of August. Tip waiters about 5 per cent over the included service charge (*coperto*).

Artisanal *linguini* for sale

Meal prices

Prices at Italian restaurants can vary widely in price. You will find everything from value-for-money finds to five-star dining blowouts. Prices in this guide are subject to fluctuation and should be used only as a rough guide.

★ Under €50
★★ €50–€80
★★★ €80–€150
★★★★ Over €150

Aosta
La Cave de Tillier Ristorante Brasserie ★
Gnocchi fonduta – tender potato pasta in a creamy fontina cheese sauce – is a speciality.
Via de Tillier 40. Tel: (016) 523 0133.
Ristorante Praetoria ★
The rabbit is excellent, as is the cheese-filled *ravioli*.
Via San Anselmo 9. Tel: (0165) 443 56.

Bergamo (Città Alta)
Angelo Mangili
Shop here for foods to take home: local cheeses, salami, ham, dried pasta and ingredients for the local *polenta*.
Via Gombito 8. Tel: (035) 248 774.
Caffè del Tasso ★
The best café location in town, with good pastries and a piano bar.
Piazza Vecchia 3. Tel: (035) 237 966.
Da Franco Ristorante ★
Lively, informal setting for well-prepared local dishes, including *caprese* salad of mozzarella and tomatoes.
Via Colleoni 8. Tel: (035) 238 565.

Taverna dei Colleoni ★★
Upmarket restaurant noted for *casoncelli*, the local meat *ravioli*.
Piazza Vecchia 7.
Tel: (035) 232 596.

Taverna della Taragna ★
Hidden behind a cheery bar, this traditional *trattoria* has no menu, prodigious portions and *polenta* worthy of sainthood.
Viale Papa Giovanni XXIII 3,
San Pellegrino.
Tel: (0345) 215 64.

Trattoria Tre Torre ★
Polenta with porcini and Taleggio cheese is a local speciality.
Piazza Mercato del Fieno (Via San Lorenzo).
Tel: (035) 244 366.

Lake Como

Albergo Ristorante Il Vapore ★
Home-made dishes and perfectly cooked lake fish.
Piazza T Grossi 3, Menaggio.
Tel: (0344) 322 29.

Alle Darsene di Loppia ★★
Overlooking the vintage lake gondolas on the Darsena just outside the back gate of the Melzi gardens, this restaurant loves contrasts: between the hip décor and warm personal service, and between the *cucina nuova* and old favourites on the menu.
Via al Porto 1, Darsena di Loppia. Tel: (031) 445 1102; www. alledarsenediloppia.com.
Open: Tue–Sun noon–2.30pm & 7–9.30pm.

Hosteria del Platano ★★
Homey, comfortable and hospitable, this restaurant will even take you to and from your hotel so you don't have to drive back after dark.
Via Statale 29, Fiumelatte. Tel: (0341) 815 215. Open: Wed–Mon noon–2.30pm & 7–9.30pm.

Il Solito Posto ★★
Delicate asparagus *ravioli* or hearty *ossobuco* in a cosy atmosphere.
Via Lambertenghi 9, Como. Tel: (031) 271 352.

Caprese salad combines tomatoes with buffalo mozzarella

La Punta ★★

As its name suggests, this restaurant sits at the tip of Bellagio, with water on three sides and a sweeping view of the lake and mountains – the perfect spot for watching evening fall and the lights twinkle around the lake. The food matches the view.
Via Eugenio Vitali 19, Bellagio. Tel: (031) 951 888; www. lapuntabellagio.com

Lake Garda
Bar Pizzeria Adria ★

Excellent *bruschetta* and light dishes served in an olive-tree shaded garden, overlooking Il Vittoriale.
Via dei Caduti 17, Gardone Sopra. Tel: (0365) 20 895.

Pizzeria La Strambata ★

Lively place for creative pizzas and generous *caprese* salads.
Via Fosse, Bardolino. Tel: (045) 721 0110.

Trattoria La Bicocca ★

Pumpkin-filled *ravioli* is the house speciality.
Vicolo Molino 6, Desenzano. Tel: (0309) 143 658.

Agli Angeli ★★★

Well known, and for good reason, this hilltop *osteria* treats each dish as a work of art – in both flavour and appearance. Their own pasta speciality is superb.
Piazza Garibaldi 2, Gardone Sopra. Tel: (0365) 20 832. Open: mid-Mar–mid-Oct Tue–Sun.

Villa del Sogno ★★★

Dinner here is a fine art, from the creative concepts to the beautiful presentation and service.
Via Zanardelli 107, Gardone Riviera. Tel: (0365) 290 181; www.villadelsogno.it

Lake Lugano
Trani ★★

Smart wine bar with delectable game and vegetarian dishes. Sample Ticino wines here.
Via Cattedrale 12, Lugano. Tel: (091) 922 0505.

Ristorante Locanda Orico ★★★

The *degustazione* menu offers six courses; the *carpaccio* is outstanding.
Via Orico 13, Bellinzona. Tel: (091) 825 1518; www.locandaorico.ch

Restaurant tables in the street

Lake Maggiore
Ristorante Belvedere ★

An airy vine-draped terrace above the lake; try tender *tortellini* filled with goat cheese.
Via Piave 11, Ranco. Tel: (0331) 975 260.

Locanda dei Mai Intees ★★

Simply the most delectable lamb you'll ever eat; the pasta chef is a genius.
Via Nobile Claudio Riva 2, Azzate (Varese). Tel: (033) 245 7223; www.mai-intees.com

Il Sole di Ranco ★★★

One of the finest dining experiences in northern Italy; this chef richly

deserves his two Michelin stars.
Piazza Venezia 5, Ranco (Angera). Tel: (0331) 976 507; www.ilsolediranco.it

Lake Orta

Albergo San Rocco ★★★
Seventeenth-century nuns chose a stunning spot for their convent, and this 21st-century restaurant has found a perfect home here overlooking the lake. The varied menu is rich in local fresh ingredients, from lake fish to truffles.
Via Gippini 11, Orta San Giulio. Tel: (0322) 911 977; www.hotelsanrocco.it

Milan

Caffè Sarducci ★
Café near Sant'Ambrogio, good bar snacks in late afternoon.

Via San Vittore 2. Tel: (02) 890 0440.

Caffè Vergnano ★
Excellent pasta dishes and sandwiches. The dining room is in the back.
Via Speronari 3 (near Duomo). Tel: (02) 8699 6858.

Trattoria Il Carpaccio ★
The kind of unpretentious restaurant you always wish for in a city and rarely find; superb *tortellini*.
Via Palazzi 9 (opposite Hotel Sanpi). Tel: (02) 2940 5982.

Caffè dell'Opera ★★
Expensive if you take a table, but a very elegant place for *gelato* or a pastry (*pasta*).
Via Manzoni 12. Tel: (02) 799 653.

Da Ilia ★★
This restaurant has been here for half a century, so it must be doing

something right.
Via Lecco 1. Tel: (02) 2952 1895; www.ristorante-ilia.it

Joia ★★
Michelin-starred restaurant with inspired vegetarian dishes and fish. One of Milan's best restaurants.
Via Panfilo Castaldi 18. Tel: (02) 2952 2124. Closed: weekends, Aug, Dec & Jan.

Pizzeria di Porta Garibaldi ★★
Their own *gnocchi* (potato dumplings), and pizza served by the slice.
Corso Como 6. Tel: (02) 655 1926.

Trattoria C'era Una Volta ★★
This restaurant is renowned for its traditional *ossobuco*.
Via Palermo 20. Tel: (02) 654 060.

Trattoria Milanese ★★
Typical Milanese dishes, including *ossobuco*.
Via Santa Marta 11. Tel: (02) 8645 1991.

La Carbonella ★★★
Look for *risotto* with white truffles from nearby Alba.
Via Terraggio 9. Tel: (02) 861 835.

Tasty treats in Milan

Monza

**Ristorante Toscano
Treppiede ★★**

Hospitable, informal,
with Tuscan menu.
*Viale Lombardia 2,
Rondo di Monza.*
Tel: (039) 360 265.

Derby Grill ★★★

Don't be misled by the
British name; this is fine
Nuovo-Italian dining.
Bookings essential.
*Via Regina Margherita
di Savoia 15.*
Tel: (039) 39 421.

Verona

Brek ★

Don't be put off by the
fact that this is a fast-food
chain. The food is good
value, the surroundings
bright and they cater for
vegetarians, who can
assemble their own salads
and stir-fry combos.
Piazza Bra 20.
Tel: (045) 800 4561.

Osteria del Duca ★

Local favourite for pasta
and vegetable dishes, veal
carpaccio with arugula,
and snails with *polenta*.
Via Arche Scaligere 2.
Tel: (045) 594 474.

Le Petarine ★

Osteria serving home-
made seasonal specialities

like tripe soup.
Via San Mamaso 6.
Tel: (045) 594 453.

Osteria Sottoriva ★/★★

Cosy tables are sheltered
by a medieval arcade, for
a low-key atmosphere; the
food is dependably good.
Via Sottoriva 9a.
Tel: (045) 801 4323.
Closed: Wed.

Osteria Sgarzerie ★★

Ossobuco alla milanese
(braised veal shanks) or
the *ravioli de zucco* with
butter and sage are good
choices, but you can't go
wrong with anything on
the menu.
Corte Sgarzerie.
Tel: (045) 800 0312.

Ristorante Greppia ★★

Summer dining on the
piazzetta (small piazza);
pasta stuffed with

The daily menu is usually
posted outside

pumpkin, and hard-to-
find Venetian dishes.
*Vicolo Samaritana 3 (off
Via Mazzini).*
*Tel: (045) 800 4577; www.
ristorantegreppia.com*

Trattoria alla Pigna ★★

Creative dishes such as
steelhead trout with a
brandy and courgette
flowers sauce; the menu
is translated.
Via Pigna 4.
Tel: (045) 800 4080.

Due Torri ★★★

Impeccable service in a
former *palazzo*; dishes
include *risotto* with
pignoli (pine nuts) and
gorgonzola sauce, or
lamb chops with mixed
wild berries.
Piazza Sant'Anastasia 4.
Tel: (045) 595 044.

Ristorante Arquade ★★★

Choose the market
tasting menu (a menu
based on what is in the
market that day), with
accompanying wines, to
sample the breadth of
this brilliant chef's
talents and the scope of
the villa's famed wine
cellars.
*Villa del Quar, Via Quar
12, Pedemonte (Verona).*
*Tel: (045) 680 0681;
www.hotelvilladelquar.it*

Savouring local wines

The soils of Lombardy and the neighbouring regions of Piedmont and Veneto are perfect for wine production. Deep, sweet calcareous earth is drenched with plenty of sunshine and enough water to produce the best wine grapes. Long known for their good, reliable wines, vintners have recently become more sophisticated, creating even finer wines while retaining the unique essence of these lands. Local connoisseurs were quick to appreciate this, and the better local restaurants have wine lists that run to pages of such wines. Even in neighbourhood *trattorie*, the *vino di tavola* (house wine) served by the carafe (*vino sfuso*,

Valpolicella grapes ready for harvest

literally 'loose' or from the barrel) is almost certain to be of a good quality.

From the Piedmont, west of Milan, look for the Barbaresco, Barbera d'Alba and Barolo reds, and Gavi or Roero Arneis whites. From the eastern shores of Lake Garda come the hearty Bardolino and the lighter Valpolicella, both reds. From Soave, just east of Verona, come delicate and light whites. The vineyards of Lombardy produce the dry red Botticino and Cellatica, and the softer and more perfumed Gropello. Capriano del Colle is pressed in both a red and a white.

Franciacorta in Lombardy, south of Lake Iseo, has one of the newest and most exciting DOC (*denominazione di origine controllata*, or registered domaine) regions. Look for the term *Franciacorta DOCG* (the 'G' stands for 'guaranteed') on the labels of sparkling wine. The strict rules of DOCG limit production – they require that grapes are placed into small containers, that only Chardonnay or Pinot Blanc grapes are used, and that the wine is produced by secondary bottle fermentation only. Look also for the equally excellent *Franciacorta DOC* whites – straw coloured, dry and

Roadside sign advertising wine for sale

velvety – and the DOC reds, which are vivid in colour, and fruity.

Tourist offices often have brochures identifying wineries in each region, and many have wine trail maps. Use these or watch for the signs to direct you to a winery that offers tastings in their *cantina* (cellar). In some wine shops you can view the wine-making process, but you won't find the whole neighbourhood 'treading' the grapes now that the process is mechanised. Some of the more prestigious wineries ask that you phone ahead since they prepare food to accompany a tasting and even – like the outstanding Bertani winery in Novare – arrange for you to tour the interior of the villa (*see p143*). Expect to pay based on the type of experience – more for a formal tasting than for a drop-in *cantina*.

Wine bars

A good way to sample a variety of local wines is at a wine bar – *enoteca* or *osteria* – where a wide selection

is served by the glass. These establishments usually also offer a board of local artisan cheeses, a good accompaniment to wines of the same *terroir* (growing environment). These generally open late afternoon or early evening and close between midnight and 2am.

Enoteca Segreta
Vicolo Samaritana 10, Verona.
Tel: (045) 801 5824.

Lostrano Bar
Via Adamo del Pero 8, Como.
Tel: (031) 249 429.

Monti's Café
Via A Volta 47, Azzate (Lake Varese, near Maggiore). Tel: (0332) 458 583.

Osteria del Gallo
Via Vitani 20, Verona.

Osteria Panesalame
Via Marocco 22, Riva del Garda.
Tel: (0464) 551 954.

Local wines at a pavement market

Hotels and accommodation

Milan has some of Italy's most stylish and best-designed hotels, while overlooking the lakes are the grand resort hotels and historic villas (see pp176–7), as well as plenty of attractive, smaller hotels and bed and breakfasts.

A hotel in Italy is usually just that – a building with corridors of guest rooms, usually with a restaurant. Beyond that, designations are less clear. A small *albergo* may resemble a *locanda*, although the latter is usually a nice country home turned into an inn.

One way to assure a level of quality is to book through affinity groups (these differ from hotel chains) such as Best Western or Space Hotels. These are independently owned hotels with equal standards, and directories and websites with photographs. Italy's own star system is based on regular inspections. You can expect two-star hotels to have private bathrooms, three-star to have in-room telephones and television.

In Milan, consider location. For instance, the area around Stazione Centrale can be quite unsavoury, but the many good hotels there are convenient for those arriving by train or air. Using taxis after dark is not a bad idea if staying in this part of town.

Establish the rate when reserving a hotel room, and request fax or email confirmation. Always have confirmed bookings for August, Easter week, and arrival and departure nights. Some lake hotels are closed from November to March.

HOTEL GROUPS

Best Western
www.bestwestern.it
Australia *(1 800) 131 779*
Ireland *(800) 709 101*
New Zealand *(0800) 237 893*
South Africa *(0800) 994 284*
UK *(08457) 737 373*
USA *(1 800) 780 7234*

The Charming Hotels
www.thecharminghotels.com
UK *(0800) 2427 6464*

Space Hotels
www.spacehotels.it
UK *(0500) 303 030*
USA/Canada *(1 800) 843 3311*
Italy *(800) 813 013*

Relais & Châteaux
www.relaischateaux.com
UK *(0800) 2000 00 02*
USA/Canada *(1 800) 735 2478*

CAMPING AND HOSTELS

Lake Garda's southern shore is ringed by large campsites catering mostly for families, with good recreational facilities and beaches. But, surprisingly, Milan itself offers a good camping option, too (*see p178*). Verona offers several choices of hostels.

Campeggio Città di Milano
Wooded tent pitches and 30 cabins.
Via G Airaghi 61, Milan. Tel: (02) 4820 7017; www.campingmilano.it

Camping Cappuccini
Tent and caravan pitches with a beach.
Via Arrigo Boito 2, Peschiera del Garda. Tel: (045) 755 1592; www.camp-cappuccini.com

Camping Castel San Pietro
Shaded riverside pitches for tents; no caravan hook-ups.
Via Castel San Pietro 2, Verona. Tel: (045) 592 037; www.campingcastelsanpietro.com

Casa della Giovane
This Catholic-run hostel is close to Verona's centre.
Via Pigna 7, Verona. Tel: (045) 596 880; www.casadellagiovane.com

Ostello Villa Francescatti
Combined hostel and camping, walking distance from the centre of Verona.
Salita Fontana del Ferro 15, Verona. Tel: (045) 590 360; fax: (045) 800 9127.

HOTELS
Aosta
Hotel Europe
Very attractive hotel in the historic centre (you can walk to major sights and the railway station), with pleasant, helpful staff, and covered parking.
Piazza Narbonne 8, 11100 Aosta. Tel: (0165) 236 363; fax: (0165) 405 66.

Bergamo
Best Western Premier Cappello D'Oro
In the centre near railway and funicular stations; covered parking. Full English breakfast buffet.
Viale Papa Giovanni XXIII 12, 24121 Bergamo. Tel: (035) 232 503; fax: (035) 242 946; www.bestwestern.it

Hotel Agnello d'Oro
High in the old city, charming, comfortable and only steps away from all the sights.
Via Gombito 22, 24121 Bergamo. Tel: (035) 249 883; fax: (035) 235 612.

Lake Como
Grand Hotel Tremezzo Palace
Belle Époque splendour on the lake, backed by beautiful gardens.
Via Regina 8, Tremezzo. Tel: (034) 442 491; fax: (034) 440 201.

Grand Hotel sign in Stresa

Grand Hotel Villa Serbelloni

The star of Lake Como, this grand hotel combines splendour and grace with warm hospitality. Classical musicians play in the evening. Well worth a splurge.

Via Roma 1, Bellagio. Tel: (031) 950 216; www.villaserbelloni.it

Hotel Metropole & Suisse au Lac

Prime location on the waterfront. Off-season specials are a real bargain.

Piazza Cavour 19, Como. Tel: (031) 269 444; fax: (031) 300 808; www. hotelmetropolesuisse.com

Terminus

Freshly renovated Belle Époque grand hotel on the main *piazza* at the boat landing.

Lungo Lario Trieste, Como. Tel: (031) 329 111; fax: (031) 302 550; www.hotelterminus-como.com

Lake Garda

Grand Hotel Gardone

Elegant, old-fashioned hotel on a grand scale, on the lake.

Via Zanardelli 84, 25083 Gardone Riviera. Tel: (0365) 202 61; fax: (0365) 226 95; www.grangardone.it

Hotel Capri

Contemporary rooms with balconies.

Via Mirabello 21, 37011 Bardolino. Tel: (0457) 210 106; fax: (0456) 212 088; www.hotel-capri.com

Hotel Europa

Well-designed hotel in the centre of town.

Piazza Catena 9, 38066 Riva. Tel: (0464) 555 433; fax: (0464) 521 777; www.hoteleuropariva.it

Hotel Garni Diana

Modern and bright hotel with a pool, a short walk to the lake.

Via Scuisse 8, 37018 Malcesine. Tel: (0457) 500 192; fax: (0457) 400 415; www.malcesine.com/ diana

Hotel Vittorio

Art Deco hotel with bright, pleasant rooms, most with balconies. Stunning lake views.

Via Porto Vecchio 4, 25015 Descenzano. Tel: (0309) 912 245; fax: (0309) 912 270; www.hotelvittorio.it

Lake Lugano

Hotel de la Paix

Balconies overlook the lake and mountains.

Via Cattori 18, 6900 Lugano (Switzerland). Tel: +41 (091) 960 6060; fax: (091) 960 6066; www.delapaix.ch

Lake Maggiore

Best Western Hotel Milano

Very attractive hotel with friendly staff, on the lake with dockage and terrace restaurant.

Via Sempione 4, 28832 Belgirate-Novara. Tel: (0322) 765 25; fax: (0322) 762 95; www.bestwestern.it

Best Western Villa Carlotta

Large lake-shore villa with fine gardens and attractive rooms with internet points; often hosts large coach groups.

Via Sempione 121/125, 28832 Belgirate. Tel: (0322) 764 61; fax: (0322) 767 05; www.bestwestern.it

Grand Hotel des Îles Borromées

One of northern Italy's most renowned luxury

hotels, situated in a lush park overlooking the islands.

Lungolago Umberto, Stresa. Tel: (0323) 938 938; fax: (0323) 324 05; www.borromees.it

Lake Orta
Hotel San Rocco

Elegant rooms, smashing lake views, an attentive staff and an excellent restaurant.

Via Gippini 11, Orta San Giulio. Tel: (0322) 911 977; www.hotelsanrocco.it

Milan
Antica Locanda Leonardo

Small inn with excellent central location, congenial owners, and parking.

Corso Magenta 78, 20123 Milano. Tel: (02) 4801 4197; fax: (02) 4801 9012; www. anticalocandaleonardo.com

Hotel Ariston

Modern, comfortable and handily located. Bicycles are available to borrow.

Largo Carrobbio 2, 20123 Milano. Tel: (02) 7200 0556; www.aristonhotel.com

Hotel Mediolanum

Attractive modern hotel,

near the Stazione Centrale.

Via Mauro Macchi 1 (at Via Napo Torriani), 20124 Milano. Tel: (02) 670 5312; fax: (02) 6698 1921; www. mediolanumhotel.com

Hotel Sanpi Milano

Renovated, upmarket rooms, each unique. The charming courtyard is a rare oasis.

Via Lazzaro Palazzi 18, 20124 Milano. Tel: (02) 2951 3341; fax: (02) 2940 2451; www.hotelsanpimilano.it

Hotel Spadari al Duomo

A few steps from Piazza Duomo, the rooms are decorated by notable Italian artists.

Via Spadari 11, 20123 Milano. Tel: (02) 7200 2371; fax: (02) 861 184; www.spadarihotel.com

Milan/Malpensa Airport
First Hotel Malpensa Airport

Pleasant rooms, and free shuttles to flight terminals, plus a helpful staff.

Via Baracca 34, Case Nuove, Somma Lombardo. Tel: (0331)

Art Deco Hotel Vittorio in Descenzano del Garda

717 045; fax: (0331) 230 827; www.firsthotel.it

Verona
Due Torri Hotel Baglioni

A beautifully maintained palace with period antiques and providing impeccable service.

Piazza Sant'Anastasia 4, 37138 Verona. Tel: (045) 595 0444; www.baglionihotels.com

Hotel Aurora

Renovated rooms; terrace bar overlooks the market.

Piazza delle Erbe, 37138 Verona. Tel: (045) 594 717/597 834; www.hotelaurora.biz

Hotel San Luca

The 36-room hotel is a few steps from Piazza Bra, with covered parking and internet access.

Vicolo Volto San Luca 8. Tel: (045) 591 333; www.hotelsanluca.it

Living in a villa

The next best thing to owning your own villa with a view over an Italian lake is to be a guest in someone else's. This is quite possible, since the owners of many of these historic villas have turned them into small hotels, nearly always with a notable restaurant.

Villas are smaller and more personal than hotels. Their architecture is distinguished, each room different in its shape, furnishings, décor and character. The villas are usually the hosts' ancestral home; you really are a guest in a private house. Most of all, each has a history, often of several hundred years, and staying in one gives you a glimpse of those past centuries. The setting might be in a village or leafy neighbourhood of a small city, in gardens on the lake shore or surrounded by the villa's own vineyards. The dining rooms are in the hands of highly rated chefs who have won prestigious awards and stars. Most villas also have distinguished wine cellars.

Il Sole di Ranco

Elegant rooms are styled in soft colours, with full-length windows overlooking gardens and Lake Maggiore. The villa's vine-draped terrace is the place to watch the sunset reflected in the lake's waters. Day begins with breakfast breads baked in the villa's highly praised restaurant.

Piazza Venezia 5, 21020 Ranco (Varese). Tel: (0331) 976 507; fax: (0331) 976 620; www.ilsolediranco.it

Guest room in La Villa, Hotel de la Ville in Monza

La Villa, Hotel de la Ville

A distinguished former private home adjacent to the luxury boutique hotel, the villa is a secret hideaway behind its fence. Breathtakingly elegant rooms, rich in architectural detail, are furnished with fine art and antiques. Every amenity is provided, including a small TV screen beside the bathroom mirror, and a private lounge downstairs for villa guests.

Viale Regina Margherita 15, 20052 Monza. Tel: (039) 39 421; fax: (039) 367 647; www.hoteldelaville.com

Locanda dei Mai Intees

On the dining-room walls there are medieval frescoes discovered during the restoration of the manor, which was built in the 1400s. Rooms are decorated in rich Renaissance colours and antique furnishings, but the stylish marble baths are strictly 21st century. Hospitable owner Carlotta Pomati's heart is in the villa's kitchen, and it shows.

Via Nobile Claudio Riva 2, 21002 Azzate (Varese). Tel: (0332) 457 223; fax: (0332) 459 339.

Villa del Quar

The noble wine estate, surrounded by Valpolicella vineyards, is an Italian National Monument. When torchieres (large holders for torches used on the outside of buildings) and other historic

Terrace of Villa del Sogno in Gardone Riviera

details of their Renaissance ancestral home have needed replacing, the owners have commissioned handmade replicas. The airy guest rooms are a seamless blend of antique detail and mod cons, and the terrace café looks out at a clover-shaped swimming pool at the edge of a vineyard.

Via Quar 12, 37020 Pedemonte (Verona). Tel: (045) 680 0681; fax: (045) 680 0604; www.hotelvilladelquar.it

Villa del Sogno

In its own hillside park of exotic trees, this Art Nouveau villa looks down over the lake. The spacious terrace is the size of a village *piazza*, a good place to enjoy an evening aperitif or the outstanding breakfast buffet. There are matching suites of richly inlaid furniture in the guest rooms.

Via Zanardelli 107, 25083 Gardone Riviera. Tel: (0365) 290 181; fax: (0365) 290 230; www.villadelsogno.it

Practical guide

Arriving

Entry requirements

EU citizens can enter Italy for an unlimited stay with a valid passport. US, Australian, Canadian and New Zealand passport holders must have passports that are valid for at least three months from the entry date for up to 90-day stays without a visa. Reasonable amounts of tobacco, alcohol and personal belongings are tax-free.

By air

Two large airports serve Milan. **Linate** (*Tel: (02) 7485 2200*) is near the city and **Malpensa** (*Tel: (02) 7485 2200*) is halfway between Milan and Lake Maggiore – a good starting place for the lakes. Express buses connect Malpensa with at least one city on each major lake. Both airports are connected to the city centre by regular transport.
Linate: Bus No 73 to San Babila metro.
Malpensa: Express trains and buses to Stazione Centrale train station.
www.sea-aeroportimilano.it

By rail

Milan's Stazione Centrale railway station is on the M3 (yellow) metro line, four stops from Piazza Duomo. Trains to Lakes Como, Maggiore and Garda leave from this station. There is a taxi rank just outside the station; the minimum charge of about €4 increases at night, on holidays and for luggage. The Stazione Centrale area is not the best place to wander around at night.

Camping

Campsites, found all over the lakes region, are most plentiful around southern Lake Garda (*www.gardacamp.com*). Most could barely accommodate a caravan, although a few sites are more suitable for a camping holiday, such as the park-like **3Lago Camping** on tiny Lago di Ghirla, between Lakes Maggiore and Lugano (*Via Trelago 20, Ghirla (Varese). Tel: (0332) 716 583; www.3lagocamping.com*). In Milan, **Campeggio Città di Milano** offers tent pitches and sports facilities (*Via Airaghi 61. Tel: (02) 4820 7017. Metro: De Angeli, then bus No 72*). Tourist office accommodation directories usually include lists of campsites.

Children

Italians, as a rule, adore children, and, although they do not often travel with their own, they are highly tolerant of other people's. Bring child car seats to avoid the extra charge many car rental companies add – if they are available at all. Hotels and other accommodation usually supply a baby cot or rollaway bed if asked when booking.

Milan is difficult for parents of infants and toddlers because of the stairs in metro stations; and you must collapse pushchairs on trams and buses. However, locals will be quick to help. Only an occasional restaurant will have high chairs – best to tuck a collapsible seat into the pushchair pocket. (*See also pp158–9.*)

Climate

The Alps to the north of the region moderate summer heat (although it is still hot), while the lake waters moderate the winters. Mountain-sheltered western shores have created mild microclimates where tropical plants grow, north of their usual range. While showers are common in spring, autumn and winter, snow accumulations on the lake shores are rare. Sunshine averages three to four hours daily in winter and more than nine in summer. Summer is brutally hot in Milan and the Po Valley; winters (December to February) are surprisingly cool, with snow, fog and rain.

Consulates

Australia
Via Borgogna 2. Tel: (02) 7770 4117.
Canada
Via Vittor Pisani 19. Tel: (02) 675 81.
New Zealand
Via Guido d'Arezzo 6.
Tel: (02) 4801 2544.
South Africa
Via San Giovanni sul Muro 4.
Tel: (02) 809 036.
UK
Via San Paolo 7. Tel: (02) 733 001.

USA
Via Principe Amadeo 2/10.
Tel: (02) 290 351.

Crime

Pickpockets, purse-snatchers and car thieves are the biggest safety worry for travellers in northern Italy, especially in Milan. But the number of police in Stazione Centrale shows how seriously the city authorities take their recent crackdown. Keep handbags and cameras in your hand or hidden, never hanging loose. Savvy women do not carry handbags at all, stowing guidebooks and personal effects in a tote, and keeping money, documents and credit cards in a hidden wallet. Men should also use hidden wallets, and never carry one in a rear pocket that can be easily slit from the bottom.

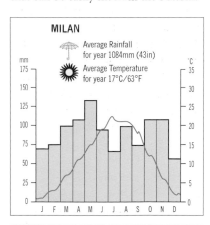

WEATHER CONVERSION CHART
25.4mm = 1 inch
°F = 1.8 × °C + 32

Lock cars and hide tourist items, such as maps or guidebooks, so that thieves won't assume there to be luggage in the car boot. If a robbery does occur, report it immediately to the police, to support insurance claims. Carrying identification, such as a passport, is required by law.

Driving
Car hire
Book car hire well in advance since cars are seldom available without a reservation. The lowest rates are frequently in a package with air fare, booked through the airline. Often, you must purchase the collision damage waiver insurance cover, which is not included in Italy, adding another expense to car hire. If you live outside Europe, you can avoid this by leasing a car. Renault Eurodrive has a very smooth system for this, completing the paperwork in advance and meeting you with a brand-new car at Milan airport.

Rates compare favourably with rentals (and without added VAT), and drivers over 70 are not banned, as they are by most rental agencies. *Renault Eurodrive. US (800) 221 1052; www.renaultusa.com. France (0) 505 1515.*

Documents and insurance
EU and US drivers need only their own current driving licence; other travellers should also carry an International Driving Permit, obtained in your own country, usually through an automobile club. You must have registration and insurance documents in the car at all times. It is also important to get a card from your insurer to prove that you have third-party coverage.

Driving conditions
The main east–west motorway (*autostrada*) is the A-4 between Milan and Venice, which passes close to the cities in this book and to the shore of Lake Garda. Once you overcome your

You can cruise on all the major lakes

initial horror at the way Italian drivers weave between cars at high speeds, the A-4 is not unlike motorways anywhere. More disconcerting are the winding mountain roads, often with steep drops and no guard rails. Don't be surprised to meet cars rounding tight corners at least halfway across your lane. Stay alert and defensive, eyes on the road at all times, and avoid these roads in rain, in winter and at night.

Finding your way

Route numbers are not always on road signs, so look for signposts pointing to towns and cities on your route. It is important to know the destination city of an *autostrada* in each direction, since the motorways are not labelled by compass points. The A-26 to Lake Maggiore is signposted to Gravellona, a tiny town at the Swiss border. This system can be quite puzzling when trying to determine which *autostrada* entrance to take.

When asking directions, watch as well as listen to the reply, since directions will all be accompanied by helpful hand gestures. *Sempre diritto* means 'straight ahead' and *semaforo* is a traffic light. *Segnale* is a signpost and *rotatoria* is a roundabout.

Breakdowns and accidents

If you have a breakdown, pull over and place a warning triangle 100m (110yds) behind the vehicle. You must also wear an orange safety vest – all hire cars come with both the triangle and the vest, but if driving your own car you must bring them with you. Then dial 116 for assistance or flag down another driver with a mobile phone. The tow truck driver will probably not speak English, but will have a multilingual auto parts manual. You will have to pay for towing and parts. Members of automobile clubs in their own country can usually arrange for cover; ask your local automobile club about a letter of introduction or ETI booklet.

In the event of an accident, remain at the scene until police arrive, stay calm and request an English-speaking interpreter before making a statement.

Fuel

Petrol (unleaded is *benzina senza piombo*) and diesel are sold by the litre. Many stations are self-service, using credit cards at the pump, but some smaller stations require cash. Be sure to keep your tank full on weekends, since many stations close then.

Right-hand driving

In Italy, all traffic drives on the right, which is a problem for those from the UK and other left-hand drive countries. The most difficult moments are when you start out each day, especially if you enter a road or street without traffic. Solve this by using some sort of sign to alert you each time you enter the car.

Traffic regulations

The left lane of an *autostrada* is only for passing, and other vehicles must keep to the right. If a driver approaching from behind in the same lane flashes high beams, you are expected to move to the right as soon as you can. Do not pass on the right.

Rules at intersections and roundabouts will seem familiar, except that they are backwards for those used to driving on the left. When there is no other indication, the vehicle on the right has the right of way, except at a roundabout. There a vehicle in the circle has the right of way over entering traffic. A green arrow indicating a left turn means only that turning is allowed, not that oncoming traffic is stopped by a red light.

Speed limits

Although rarely observed by locals, the speed limit on an *autostrada* is 130km/h (81mph). Lower limits are posted when the road is dangerous or in urban areas (usually 100km/h/ 62mph) or in a construction zone (*zona cantiere*), where you are required by law to slow down. In towns, the limit is 50km/h (30mph), and residential areas often post speed limits of 30km/h (20mph). The maximum speed on rural roads is 90km/h (55mph); be especially careful when these go through the centre of villages, where blind bends can hide all sorts of perils. The speed limit for caravans over 3,550kg (3.5 tonnes) and camper vans is 100km/h (62mph) on *autostrade*, 80km/h (50mph) elsewhere, and 50km/h (31mph) in towns.

Drinking and driving

Italy has strict laws limiting a driver's permissible blood alcohol level to 0.08 per cent. Exceed this and risk stiff penalties – as well as an accident. A driver with an illegal level also risks being automatically held at fault in any accident.

Seat belts

Seat belts are mandatory for driver and all passengers, whether in the front or back seats. Children under 12 must be in the back seat.

Tolls

Most *autostrade* charge tolls. Normally you take a ticket at the beginning and pay at the end, using cash or a bank or credit card. Be careful to find the right exit booth, and be aware that using a credit card requires a PIN number.

Electricity

Italy operates at 220 volts. UK appliances will work, but require an adaptor to the European plug with two round prongs. American appliances need a transformer and an adaptor.

Emergency telephone numbers

Police (*carabinieri*) *Tel: 112.*
Emergencies (*pronto soccorso*) *Tel: 113.*
Automobile Club d'Italia (ACI)
Breakdown service for road assistance *Tel: 116.*
Ambulance (*ambulanza*) *Tel: (02) 3883.*

Health

Public health conditions are generally good in northern Italy, but drinking water is not always safe (many travellers and locals prefer bottled water). No immunisations are required or necessary for travel. Minor medical problems are usually handled by pharmacies (*farmacie*). These take turns staying open for emergencies (*normal hours: Mon–Fri 8.30am–12.30pm & 4.30–7pm*). Each pharmacy posts a sign outside telling of the nearest open pharmacy. The one on the first floor of Stazione Centrale is open 24 hours (be sure to use a taxi at night). For more serious illnesses or injury, a tourist office or hotel can suggest English-speaking doctors. Bring enough prescription medications for the entire trip, with a copy of the prescription in generic form, plus aspirin, which is available only in pharmacies in Italy.

Insurance

Experienced travellers carry insurance to cover their belongings and cost of the trip. Travel insurance should include provision for cancelled or delayed flights, as well as immediate transportation home in the case of medical emergency. EU citizens are entitled to free emergency medical care in a public hospital. Showing a passport might be enough, but you should carry an EHIC card (UK travellers get one from the post office, by phoning *0845 606 2030* or at *www.ehic.org.uk*). Non-EU citizens are covered only if they have travel medical insurance.

Lost property

Milan's *Ufficio Oggetti Rinvenuti* (Lost Property Office) holds items found in public transport or stations, as well as documents and passports found on the street and put in letter boxes (*Via Friuli 30. Tel: (02) 8845 3907. Open: Mon–Fri 8.30am–4pm*). Property lost on trains is kept at Stazione Centrale, in the *Deposito Bagagli* (Left Luggage Office), next to Information. Another place to check for lost documents is at the postal *Ufficio Oggetti Rinvenuti* (*Via Ferrante Aporti. Tel: (02) 669 0658*). To check on lost luggage call the relevant airport (*Malpensa. Tel: (02) 5858 0070. Linate. Tel: (02) 7012 4451*).

Maps

The most up-to-date and reliable road maps are published by **Touring Club Italiano** (*www.touringclub.it*) and by **Automobile Club d'Italia (ACI)**. It helps to have one with topography, since what looks like a short cut might go over a mountain. *Automobile Club d'Italia (ACI), Via Marsala 8, 00185*

Milan's public places are well patrolled by police

Roma. Tel: (06) 49 981; fax: (06) 499
8234; www.aci.it

Media

English-language daily newspapers are
available at larger newsstands. The most
useful local newspaper for travellers is
Corriere della Serra, for its 'Milan'
section listing concerts and events.
Published monthly, Hello Milano is
distributed by the tourist office, with
events and museum hours, nightlife
and local insider information.

Money matters

The euro (pronounced 'arrow' in Italy) is
the currency, and exchange facilities are
near airport arrival gates; Malpensa's are
open 24 hours. In terms of fees and
value, though, ATMs are often better.

Avoid carrying large amounts of
cash, or hide it well. Traveller's cheques
must usually be cashed at banks,
although very few banks offer this
service now; credit or debit cards are
easier. If possible, bring at least one
major credit card – Visa is the most
commonly accepted. Some small
businesses – agritourism lodgings,
family restaurants and some small
hotels – do not accept them, but most
places do.

Cash machines (bancomat) have the
best exchange rates and are everywhere.
Check with your card issuer to find out
which network to use and be sure that
your PIN number can be used abroad.
A bank debit card that draws directly on
your account usually costs less for cash

advances than a credit card, but either
assures the best exchange rate.

Banks are usually open
Monday–Friday 8.30am–1pm or
1.30pm, sometimes reopening for an
hour in the afternoon and staying open
later on Thursday. Stock up on euros
before weekends because banks are
closed and cash machines may be out
of money, or out of order.

Opening times

Expect all but the large museums, shops
and offices to close at midday, although
this is slowly changing. Closing times
vary between noon and 1pm, and
reopening is most often at 2pm or 3pm,
but may be later, especially in the
summer. Churches are notoriously
irregular in their opening hours, but
the most common hours are 9am–1pm
and 3–7pm. Smaller museums and
attractions are also highly erratic, so
don't be surprised if they are closed
when they say they are open. Time
is not an essential word in the Italian
vocabulary.

Most shops close on Monday
mornings. Food shops usually close
Wednesday afternoons. Major city
supermarkets and petrol stations on
autostrade stay open during the middle
of the day, and some Milan stores have
done away with midday closing. In
tourist places or during the summer,
shops may remain open longer. Many
businesses and nearly all restaurants in
Milan close for the month of August,
making it a poor time to be there.

Nearly all museums and attractions, and many churches, are closed on Monday. Mondays are a good day for a driving or train tour, or to ride a mountain tramway. Cafés at the top will be open.

Police

Each town's *polizia urbana* deals with local traffic and parking, and *polizia stradale* handle highway traffic. Report thefts to a *questura* (police station) and ask for a *denuncia*, a document needed to file insurance claims. More serious crimes are handled by the *carabinieri* (military police).

Post offices

Most tourist maps note the location of the city's main post office (*ufficio postale*), or ask at your hotel. You can buy postage stamps (*francobolli*) from most newsstands.

Public holidays

1 January	**New Year's Day**
6 January	**Epiphany**
March/April	**Easter Monday**
25 April	**Liberation Day**
1 May	**Labour Day**
2 June	**Anniversary of the Republic (Republic Day)**
15 August	**Feast of the Assumption**
1 November	**All Saints' Day**
8 December	**Immaculate Conception**
25 December	**Christmas Day**
26 December	**St Stephen's Day**

Milan's modern streetcars

Practical guide

Public transport

ATM operates the metro, buses and trams, and tickets are available at newsstands, vending machines and at kiosks in some stations. Validate your ticket in the meter as you enter the vehicle or when going through the turnstile. If you plan to ride more than three times in a day, a day ticket is better value. It needs to be validated on first use. The metro runs until about midnight. If a bus does not replace the route, you can use the economical Radiobus until 2am to get from the city centre to the outer districts. *Tel: (02) 4803 4803.*

Sustainable tourism

Thomas Cook is a strong advocate of ethical and fairly traded tourism and believes that the travel experience should be as good for the places visited as it is for the people who visit them. That's why we firmly support The Travel Foundation, a charity that develops solutions to help improve and protect holiday destinations, their environment, traditions and

(*Cont. on p188*)

Language

Italian is not a difficult language. It has fewer words than many other languages, and few synonyms. Every letter is pronounced and pronunciation rules are much like English. Those who read other Romance languages, especially Spanish, will be able to read Italian. Italians are very sympathetic to foreigners who try to speak their language, and will listen patiently and appreciate your attempts. It also helps that Italians use their hands so expressively – often their sign language will carry you through when you don't understand a word. Those who deal most with travellers speak some English, but everywhere people are very pleased when you at least begin with *Buongiorno* (Good day).

PRONUNCIATION

C followed by E or I	CH	
C all other times	K	
G followed by I or E	G in George	
G all other times	G in gorge	

GG	DG in edge	
ZZ	TZ (palazzo is said 'palatzo')	
GN	NY as in canyon	
GL	LL as in medallion	

NUMBERS

1	uno	21	ventuno	
2	due	22	ventidue	
3	tre	30	trenta	
4	quattro	40	quaranta	
5	cinque	50	cinquanta	
6	sei	60	sessanta	
7	sette	70	settanta	
8	otto	80	ottanta	
9	nove	90	novanta	
10	dieci	100	cento	
11	undici	101	centuno	
12	dodici	110	centodieci	
13	tredici	200	duecento	
14	quattordici	500	cinquecento	
15	quindici	1,000	mille	
16	sedici	5,000	cinquemila	
17	diciassette	10,000	diecimila	
18	diciotto	50,000	cinquanta mila	
19	diciannove	1,000,000	un milione	
20	venti	2,000,000	due milione	

DAYS OF THE WEEK

Monday	lunedì
Tuesday	martedì
Wednesday	mercoledì
Thursday	giovedì
Friday	venerdì
Saturday	sabato
Sunday	domenica

MONTHS OF THE YEAR

January	gennaio
February	febbraio
March	marzo
April	aprile
May	maggio
June	giugno
July	luglio
August	agosto
September	settembre
October	ottobre
November	novembre
December	dicembre

WEIGHTS

$\frac{1}{2}$	un mezzo	**100gm**	un etto	**1 pound**	mezzo chilo
$\frac{1}{4}$	un quarto	**1kg**	un chilo (key-low)	**1 litre**	un litro
$\frac{1}{3}$	un terzo				

USEFUL PHRASES

yes/no	sì/no
thank you	grazie
please	per favore
you are welcome	prego
excuse me	scusi
I'm sorry	mi dispiace
I would like	vorrei
I don't understand	non capisco
I don't like that	non mi piace
I want	voglio (vol-yo)
I would prefer	preferisco
okay	va bene
big/little	grande/piccolo
hot/cold	caldo/freddo
open/closed	aperto/chiuso
right/left	destra/sinistra
good/bad	buono/cattivo
fast/slow	presto/lento
much/little	molto/poco
expensive/cheap	caro/economico
go away (as a command)	va via!
at what time	a che ora
do you speak English?	parla inglese?
where is...?	dove...? (doh-veh)
stop it	smettila
leave me alone	lasciami in pace

DRIVING

accident	l'incidente
air pressure	la pressione
breakdown	il guasto
car	la macchina
does not work	non funziona
full	pieno
ignition	l'accensione

motor	il motore
oil	l'olio
petrol/diesel	la benzina/ il gasolio
petrol station	il distributore
straight ahead	sempre diritto
turn right/left	gira a destra/ sinistra
unleaded	senza piombo
water	l'acqua

ROAD SIGNS

attenzione	watch out
deviazione	detour
divieto di accesso/ senso vietato	no entry
divieto di sosta/ sosta vietata	no parking
incrocio	crossroads
limite di velocità	speed limit
parcheggio	parking
pericolo	danger
pronto soccorso	first aid
rallentare	slow down
senso unico	one-way street
strada chiusa	road closed
strada senza uscita	dead end, cul-de-sac
tenere la destra	keep right
traffico limitato	restricted access
uscita veicoli	exit
vietato fumare	no smoking
vietato il sorpasso	no overtaking (passing)
vietato il transito	no through traffic
zona rimorchio	tow-away zone

culture. To find out what you can do to make a positive difference to the places you travel to and the people who live there, please visit *www.thetravelfoundation.org.uk*

Telephones

Make calls from public telephones with a card (*carta telefonica*) bought from any newsstand (*tabacchi*). You must use the card in a phone from that company (green cards for green phones, etc), so be sure to ask where the nearest one is when you buy a card, and buy in small denominations. On some phonecards you must snap the corner off before using it, while on others you must scrape away a coating to reveal a code.

Telephone numbers occasionally change, so, if your call does not go through, check to see if a digit has been added. Ask a tourist information centre or hotel desk to help if you cannot reach a number. Always ask for the surcharge rate before making international calls from a hotel room.

Mobile phone numbers begin with a *3*; if you see an old number with the prefix *03*, omit the zero. Your UK, New Zealand and Australian mobile phone should work in Italy; US and Canadian cell phones will not. Travellers from those countries can solve this easily by buying an Italian SIM card and paying local call costs.

To call or fax Italy from outside the country, dial international access, then the country code (*39*), then the area code without the *0*, followed by the number.

To call internationally from Italy, dial *00*, then the country code (Australia = *61*, Ireland = *353*, New Zealand = *64*, UK = *44*, US and Canada = *1*) followed by the local number, omitting the first digit if it is 1 or 0.

To access your own network, use the following direct dial numbers:
Australia: Telstra *172 1061*; Optus *172 1161*.
Canada: *172 1001*.
Ireland: *172 0353*.
New Zealand: *172 1064*.
UK: BT *172 0044*.
US: AT&T *172 1011*; MCI *172 1022*; Sprint *172 1877*.

Time

Italy is GMT plus one hour in winter, and two hours ahead from the end of March to late October. Time is not an important issue in Italy, and people may be surprised when you turn up at a set time.

Tipping

Tip waiters about 5 per cent, although most Italians simply leave between €1 and €5 on the table, depending on the establishment. In family-run restaurants, tipping is not expected, but appreciated. In cafés and bars, simply leave the small change. The modest *coperto* or cover charge at most restaurants is not for the service;

in fact, no one seems sure exactly what it is for.

Toilets

Finding a public toilet can be a challenge. On the *autostrade*, petrol stations have them. You'll also find them in museums and bus and train stations (although the latter will often not be an aesthetic experience). They are labelled *Uomini* for men and *Donne* for women. Most cafés would prefer you to buy a drink first.

Tourist information

Most towns with any tourist traffic (or hope of it) have tourist information centres, called either *Pro Loco* or *APT*. They are usually at the main railway or boat station, the main *piazza*, or near a popular attraction. Apart from those in large towns, these usually close at midday. Normal hours are Monday–Saturday 9am–1pm and 4–6pm or 7pm; shorter hours in winter, or closed. Some can make accommodation reservations, and all can suggest options. Some offices offer useful booklets of detailed dining, shopping, accommodation and attractions listings, but you usually have to request these. They are the best source of current opening hours, which change often.

Travellers with disabilities

Except in the cities, where a few places have wheelchair access, facilities for mobility-impaired travellers are

MEN'S SUITS

UK	36	38	40	42	44	46	48
Europe	46	48	50	52	54	56	58
USA	36	38	40	42	44	46	48

DRESS SIZES

UK	8	10	12	14	16	18
France	36	38	40	42	44	46
Italy	38	40	42	44	46	48
Europe	34	36	38	40	42	44
USA	6	8	10	12	14	16

MEN'S SHIRTS

UK	14	14.5	15	15.5	16	16.5	17
Europe	36	37	38	39/40	41	42	43
USA	14	14.5	15	15.5	16	16.5	17

MEN'S SHOES

UK	7	7.5	8.5	9.5	10.5	11
Europe	41	42	43	44	45	46
USA	8	8.5	9.5	10.5	11.5	12

WOMEN'S SHOES

UK	4.5	5	5.5	6	6.5	7
Europe	38	38	39	39	40	41
USA	6	6.5	7	7.5	8	8.5

poor. Airports are mostly wheelchair accessible, lake steamers usually are, and major hotels have often adapted a few rooms, but travel can be very difficult otherwise. Most museums, theatres and public buildings are not ramped. However, an occasional light shines: admission to football matches is free to people with disabilities through gates 50–51. Parking is free in special blue zones for cars with an international disabled sticker.

For current information, contact **RADAR**, *12 City Forum, 250 City Road, London EC1V 8AF. Tel: 020 7250 3222; www.radar.org.uk*

Index

Acknowledgements

Thomas Cook Publishing wishes to thank STILLMAN ROGERS for the photographs in this book, to whom the copyright belongs, except for the following images:

FOTOTECA ENIT/VITO ARCOMENO 146
WWW.FLICKR.COM 69
WORLD PICTURES 1, 5, 35, 63, 85, 112, 168
DREAMSTIME.COM 11 (Federico Donatini), 19 (Tan Wei Ming), 55 (Zanico), 135 (Gian Marco Valente)
THOMAS COOK 7, 122, 161, 180

For CAMBRIDGE PUBLISHING MANAGEMENT LTD:
Project editor: Karen Beaulah
Copy editor: Jo Osborn
Typesetter: Paul Queripel
Proofreader: Ian Faulkner

SEND YOUR THOUGHTS TO BOOKS@THOMASCOOK.COM

We're committed to providing the very best up-to-date information in our travel guides and constantly strive to make them as useful as they can be. You can help us to improve future editions by letting us have your feedback. If you've made a wonderful discovery on your travels that we don't already feature, if you'd like to inform us about recent changes to anything that we do include, or if you simply want to let us know your thoughts about this guidebook and how we can make it even better – we'd love to hear from you.

Send us ideas, discoveries and recommendations today and then look out for your valuable input in the next edition of this title.

Emails to the above address, or letters to Travellers Series Editor, Thomas Cook Publishing, PO Box 227, Coningsby Road, Peterborough PE3 8SB, UK.

Please don't forget to let us know which title your feedback refers to!